To Penny, Jack and Charlie,
with love and thanks.

Welcome to the fifth in a series of books that started with *How to Avoid a Wombat's Bum* and then continued through *Why Eating Bogeys Is Good for You, How Much Poo Does an Elephant Do?* and *Why Do Farts Smell Like Rotten Eggs?* to this one, *Why Does Ear Wax Taste So Gross?*

The more perceptive reader will have noticed a trend developing. That's right: every title relates to bodily parts/functions. But not the 'clean' ones – like arms or breathing – no, it's naughty things like bums and poo and farting and all that sort of thing.
The trouble is – and I'm letting you into a trade secret here – we're running out of (ahem) 'acceptable' naughty things to put in the titles of the books. Hence the title of this book.

Personally, I don't think ear wax tastes so gross – well, mine doesn't anyway. But my wonderful editor (who came up with the title) thinks ear wax definitely has the 'yuck' factor, especially when left for as long as a month before being picked!
Besides, my editor did give me the opportunity to come up with a better title.
Here are some of the ones I suggested:

WHY OCTOPUSES EAT THEMSELVES
THE BOY WHO PEED BEETLES
WHAT YOU WOULD WEIGH ON OTHER PLANETS
THE KING WHO HAD A SWEAR BOX
WHY YOU CAN'T SNEEZE IN YOUR SLEEP
THE MAN WHO ATE 128 BICYCLES
HOW TO ESCAPE A CROCODILE

Mitchell Symons was born in 1957 in London and educated at Mill Hill School and the LSE, where he studied law. Since leaving BBC TV, where he was a researcher and then a director, he has worked as a writer, broadcaster and journalist. He was a principal writer of early editions of the board game Trivial Pursuit and has devised many television formats. He is also the author of more than thirty books, and currently writes a weekly column for the *Sunday Express*.

www.**grossbooks**.co.uk

Also by Mitchell Symons:

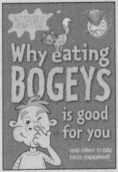

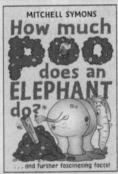

Why does EAR WAX taste so gross?*

... and more top trivia!

MITCHELL SYMONS

RED FOX

WHY DOES EAR WAX TASTE SO GROSS?
A RED FOX BOOK 978 1 862 30759 9

First published in Great Britain by Doubleday,
an imprint of Random House Children's Publishers UK
A Random House Group Company

Doubleday edition published 2009
Red Fox edition published 2010

7 9 10 8 6

Set in Optima

Red Fox Books are published by Random House Children's Publishers UK
61–63 Uxbridge Road, London W5 5SA

www.randomhousechildrens.co.uk
www.randomhouse.co.uk

Addresses for companies within The Random House Group Limited
can be found at: www.randomhouse.co.uk/offices.htm

THE RANDOM HOUSE GROUP Limited Reg. No. 954009

A CIP catalogue record for this book is available from the British Library.

Penguin Random House is committed to a sustainable future for our business,
our readers and our planet. This book is made from Forest Stewardship
Council® certified paper.

Printed and bound in Great Britain by Clays Ltd, St Ives plc

As you'll discover, all these titles – none of them as snappy as the one we went with – refer to facts in the book, which itself is a feast of trivia along the lines of *How to Avoid a Wombat's Bum* and *How Much Poo Does an Elephant Do?* I hope you enjoy reading it as much as I enjoyed compiling it.

Now for some big thank yous because without these people, this book couldn't have been written at all: (in alphabetical order) Luigi Bonomi, Lauren Buckland, Penny Chorlton, Annie Eaton, Mari Roberts and Nikalas Catlow.

In addition, I'd also like to thank the following people for their help, contributions and/or support: Gilly Adams, Paul Donnelley, Jonathan Fingerhut, Jenny Garrison, Bryn Musson, Nicholas Ridge, Charlie Symons, Jack Symons, Louise Symons, David Thomas, Martin Townsend and Rob Woolley.

If I've missed anyone out, then please know that – as with any mistakes in the book – it is, as ever, entirely down to my own stupidity.

Mitchell Symons
thatbook@mail.com

First things first

The first mobile phone text message was sent in December 1992.

Ferenc Szisz from Romania, driving a Renault, won the very first Formula One Grand Prix, held at Le Mans, France, in 1906.

Gold was the first metal to be discovered.

The first Burger King restaurant – called Insta Burger King – opened in Miami in 1954.

Lip gloss was first invented (by Max Factor in 1928) to make film actors' lips shiny.

In 1911,
Bobby Leach,
a British-born
circus star,
became the
first man* to go
over Niagara Falls
in a barrel and
survive – although
he ended up in
hospital for 23
weeks. Fifteen years
later, he died . . . after slipping
on a piece of orange peel in New Zealand.

Britain's first Tube escalator was
introduced at Earls Court in 1911.
Wooden-legged 'Bumper' Harris was
employed to travel up and down it to
prove that it was safe.

King Louis XV was the first
person to use a lift when in 1743, his 'flying
chair' carried him between the floors of his
Versailles palace.

*. . . but not the first person. That was Annie Edson Taylor, a
63-year-old teacher, in 1901.

Sir Arthur Conan Doyle, the creator of Sherlock Holmes, is credited with being the first person to introduce skiing to Switzerland.

The first elephant in England was a gift to King Henry III from the King of France in the 13th century.

The first diet soft drink, called 'The No-Cal Beverage', was launched in 1952.

Nottingham was the first city in the world to have Braille signs (for the blind) in its shopping malls.

Britain's first Indian restaurant opened more than 50 years before the first fish-and-chip restaurant.

Julian Lloyd Webber was London Underground's first official busker.

When Iceland played Estonia in 1996, Eidur Gudjohnsen became the first player to replace his father (Arnor) on the pitch during an international match. Between them, he and his dad helped Iceland to win 3–0.

In 2006 the Arctic Monkeys' first album, *Whatever People Say I Am, That's What I'm Not,* sold over a third of a million copies in its first week – making it the fastest-selling debut album in UK chart history.

In 1978 Emilio Marco Palma became the first person to be born in Antarctica.

The first automatic telephone exchange was invented in 1889 by an American undertaker, who wanted to prevent telephone operators from advising his rivals of the death of local citizens.

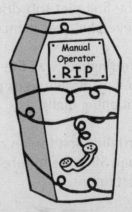

Manual Operator RIP

The first prisoner in the Tower of London – Ranulf Flambard, Bishop of Durham, in 1100 – was also the first person to escape from it. He used a rope smuggled to him by friends in a cask of wine.

Elizabeth Garrett Anderson, Britain's first female doctor, was also Britain's first female mayor (of Aldeburgh in Suffolk).

In late 17th-century Paris, lemonade became the world's first marketed soft drink.

Captain James Cook was the first man to set foot on all continents (except Antarctica).

The first message tapped by Samuel Morse over his invention the telegraph was: *What hath God wrought?*

The first words spoken by Thomas Edison over the phonograph were: *Mary had a little lamb.*

The first people to write were the Sumerians in the fourth century BC.

Rap artist Sean 'P. Diddy' Combs had his first job at age two when he modelled in an ad for Baskin-Robbins ice-cream shops.

Mauve was the first synthetic dye.

The world's first self-service restaurant, the Exchange Buffet, opened in New York in 1885. Only men were allowed to eat there.

In 1620, Dutch inventor Cornelius van Drebbel launched the world's first submarine in the Thames. The first military submarine – the Turtle – was built in 1775.

Britain's first mobile phone call was made on 1 January 1985 by Ernie Wise (of Morecambe and Wise fame).

Pamela Anderson was Canada's Centennial Baby, having been the first baby born on

the hundredth anniversary of Canada's independence.

The first instance of global electronic communications took place in 1871 when news of the Derby winner was telegraphed from London to Calcutta in under five minutes.

Pure trivia

Steven Spielberg has never had a cup of coffee in his life.

A Frenchman named Michel Lotito has eaten 128 bicycles, 15 supermarket trolleys, 6 chandeliers, 2 beds and 1 pair of skis.

Postman Pat supports Pencaster United.

The world's longest engagement lasted 67 years. Octavio Guillen and Adriana Martinez were 15 when they got engaged, and 82 on their wedding day.

Aristotle thought that blood cooled the brain.

The chihuahua is the world's smallest breed of dog, but it's named after the biggest state in Mexico.

Lord Byron had four pet geese that he took with him everywhere he went.

The NASDAQ stock exchange in New York City was totally disabled on one day in December 1987 when a squirrel burrowed through a telephone line.

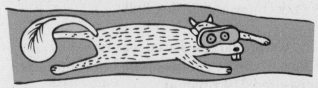

If all the Lego in the world was evenly distributed, we would each receive 30 pieces.

There is an infinite number of colours.

The people killed most often during bank robberies are the robbers.

In 1961 the Museum of Modern Art in New York City hung Matisse's *Le Bateau* upside-down for 47 days before an art student noticed the error.

It used to be against the law to slam your car door in Swiss cities.

In 1969 a Finnish farmer was cutting wood when, in the middle of a log, he found a dried fish.

Native Americans used to name their children after the first thing they saw following the birth – hence such names as Crazy Horse and Sitting Bull.

The world's largest stamp was issued by China at the beginning of the last century. It measured 210 x 65mm.

Romans used powdered mouse brains as toothpaste.

One year, Elvis Presley paid 91 per cent of his income to the US Internal Revenue Service. However, at one point in the 1960s, The Beatles were even worse off – paying more than 100 per cent tax. This meant that effectively they were paying to work.

Medieval Welsh mercenary archers only wore one shoe at a time.

Unusual museums

The Salt Museum (Northwich)

The Strawberry Museum (Wepion, Belgium)

The Norwegian Canning Museum (Stavanger, Norway)

The Sardine Museum (Sète, France)

The Toilet Seat Art Museum (San Antonio, Texas)

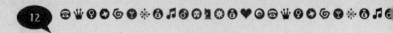

The Mustard Museum (Mount Horeb, Wisconsin)

The British Lawnmower Museum (Southport)

The Matchbox Museum (Tomar, Portugal)

The Vinegar Museum (Roslyn, South Dakota)

The Ham Museum (near Neufchâteau, France)

The Centre for Unusual Museums (Munich, Germany)

The Cumberland Pencil Museum (Keswick)

The Banana Museum (Martinique)

Banana

About average

In a lifetime, the average person will ...

... shed 57 litres of tears.

... eat 3,000 meals of spaghetti bolognese.

... eat over 13,000 eggs.

... eat 10,000 chocolate bars.

... eat 35 tons of food.

... eat 36 pigs, 36 sheep, 8 cows and over 500 chickens.

... have 7,163 baths.

... walk 100,000 miles.

... blink 500,000,000 (five hundred million) times.

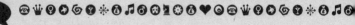
Animals

The golden bamboo lemur eats half a kilo of bamboo every day. This contains more than enough cyanide to kill a human being. No one knows why this doesn't kill the lemur. The word 'lemur' is derived from the Latin *lemures,* meaning 'spirits of the night' or 'ghosts'.

Unusually for carnivores, hyena clans are dominated by females.

Kangaroos are technically not quadrupeds but pentapeds because they use five limbs to move about – their tail being the fifth.

The raccoon derives its name from the Native American word meaning 'he who scratches with his hands'.

The beaver was originally classified as a fish because of its scaly tail.

In an experiment, rats were able to distinguish between Japanese and Dutch.

The heart of a giraffe is 60cm long, and can weigh as much as 10kg.

A male guinea pig is called a boar.

The arctic fox often follows the polar bear, feeding on the abandoned carcass of its kill.

A rat can swim for 72 hours non-stop.

Unlike most other large cats, snow leopards can't roar.

Hyenas produce an unusually high number of twins but the twins often end up fighting to the death.

Naked mole rats live longer than any other rodent – 28 years on average, which is seven times longer than ordinary mice of the same size.

The kangaroo rat doesn't drink water.

Toy-breed dogs live longer than large breeds.

Cats sleep 16 to 18 hours per day.

Chimpanzees are their own doctors: they eat rough leaves to clear parasitic worms out of their intestines.

Genetically, all living cheetahs are as close as identical twins because they are descended from a very small gene pool.

Rats can't vomit.

Car bumper stickers

CAUTION: I drive just like you!

I took an IQ test and the results were negative.

If you lived in your car, you'd be home by now.

If you don't like the way I drive, get off the pavement.

How many roads must a man travel down before he admits he is lost?

I'm not a complete idiot – some parts are missing.

He who laughs last thinks slowest.

The human body

We all have muscles
that enable us to
move our ears, but
we can no longer
make them work.

Male human brains
are about 10 per cent
heavier than female
brains.

All mammals have
jaws but only humans have chins.

There are 450 hairs in an average eyebrow.

Every square centimetre of the human body
has an average of 13 million bacteria on it.

The valves of the human heart are as thick as
a single piece of tissue paper.

One square centimetre of human skin
contains 250 sweat glands.

Human bones can withstand being squeezed twice as hard as granite can. Bones can also stand being stretched four times as hard as concrete can.

Our jaw muscles provide up to 90kg of force to bring the back teeth together for chewing.

The permanent teeth that come through to replace your baby teeth are known as succedaneous teeth.

The spinal cord is as flexible as a rubber hose.

If you are right-handed you tend to chew food on the right side of your mouth. If you are left-handed, you tend to chew on the left.

The average human body contains enough potassium to fire a toy cannon.

The largest known kidney stone weighed 1.36kg.

It takes about 20 seconds for a red blood cell to travel through the whole body.

The human heart beats once from the left-hand side and once from the right in alternate motions.

The human body contains enough carbon to make 900 pencils.

The human brain stops growing at the age of 18.

Sight accounts for 90 to 95 per cent of all sensory perceptions.

The substance that human blood resembles most closely in chemical composition is sea water.

The human body contains enough phosphorous to make 2,200 match heads.

There are 46 miles of nerves in the adult human body.

In general, girls have more tastebuds than boys.

The human brain is about 85 per cent water.

If all your DNA were stretched out, it would reach to the moon and back several thousand times.

The largest human organ is the skin, with a surface area of about 2.32 square metres.

There are more bacteria in your mouth than there are people in the world.

Around the world

Australia has more British migrants than any other country.

There is approximately one library book for every person on earth.

The town of Churchill in Manitoba, Canada, has a 20-cell prison for polar bears that cause trouble. The most frequent reason for imprisonment is scavenging in the town's rubbish dump. When a bear is released from prison, a green button is tagged behind its ear. If the bear returns to town, it's given a red button. If a red-buttoned bear attempts to come back, it's shot on sight.

There are more cows in the world than there are cars: 1.5 billion cows compared to 1 billion cars.

Half of all Dutch adults have never flown in a plane.

The longest road tunnel in the world is in Laerdal, Norway. Opened in 2000, it's over 15 miles long.

No building is taller than the tallest palm tree anywhere in the South Pacific.

India has about a quarter of the world's estimated 1.5 billion cows.

Approximately one-third of the world's population is under 18.

There are twice as many bicycles in the world as cars.

The Scandinavian languages have two 'genders', one for living things and the other for all the rest.

Some African languages have up to 20 'genders'.

30 per cent of Chinese adults live with their parents.

If you fly from Tokyo to Honolulu at 7 a.m., you'll arrive at your destination at 4.30 p.m. the previous day.

The world spends more than $2 billion a day on weaponry.

There are only 18 countries richer than Bill Gates.

Starbucks buys up 2 per cent of the world's coffee.

The Ainu – native Japanese people – believe that the world is supported on the back of a giant trout. For this reason, they have a fear of large lakes.

Announcements made by airline staff

'Welcome aboard. To operate your seat belt, insert the metal tab into the buckle, and pull tight. It works just like every other seat belt; and if you don't know how to operate one, you probably shouldn't be out in public unsupervised.'

(On a flight with no assigned seating) 'People, people, we're not picking out furniture here, find a seat and get in it!'

'Ladies and gentlemen, we've reached cruising altitude and will be turning down the cabin lights. This is for your comfort and to enhance the appearance of your flight attendants.'

'In the event of a sudden loss of cabin pressure, masks will descend from the ceiling. Stop screaming, grab the mask and pull it over your face. If you have a small child travelling with you, secure your mask before

assisting with theirs. If you are travelling with more than one small child, pick your favourite.'

'Your seat cushions can be used for flotation; and, in the event of an emergency water landing, please paddle to shore and take them with our compliments.'

'As you exit the plane, make sure to gather all of your belongings. Anything left behind will be distributed evenly among the flight attendants. Please do not leave children or spouses.'

'Ladies and gentlemen, if you wish to smoke, the smoking section on this airplane is on the wing, and if you can light 'em, you can smoke 'em.'

Creepy crawlies

Bees can recognize human faces.

There are 350,000 known species of beetle – with millions more waiting for names.

The giant cricket eats human hair.

Butterfly hunters in the 19th century used to line their top hats with cork so they had somewhere to pin the butterflies they'd caught.

Female scorpions sometimes eat their own offspring.

The average spider will spin more than four miles of silk in a lifetime.

One in four creatures on earth is a beetle.

In Britain in the past 10 years, farmland butterflies have declined by 30 per cent.

Insect flatulence – that's farting to you and me – accounts for up to a fifth of all the methane emissions on the planet.

Fire ants have adapted to cope with flooding. When water levels in their nests rise, they form a huge ball with the workers on the outside and the queen inside. This ball then floats to higher ground, where they wait for the water to go down.

The male scorpion fly gets other males to bring him food by imitating the sound of a female fly.

Some moths survive by drinking the salty tears of cattle.

Fish

There are about 21,000 varieties of fish on earth.

The Dover sole uses the sound of the wind above the waves to know where it is and where it's going.

The oldest known goldfish was Goldie, who lived for 45 years after being won at a fairground in 1960.

Mudfish can survive in mud for a year until

the rain comes.

If a goldfish is exposed to a loud noise, it can take a month for its hearing to get back to normal.

Three-quarters of a fish is eaten – the rest is used to make things such as glue, soap, margarine and fertilizer.

An electric eel can produce an average of 400 volts. Its electric organs make up four-fifths of its body.

The flounder swims sideways.

Swordfish can heat up their eyeballs to help them see when they go hunting.

Even though cuttlefish are colour-blind, they can change colour to camouflage themselves.

The bream, a freshwater fish, hatches its eggs in its mouth.

When common eels lay their eggs, they die.

The UK

0.9 per cent of the land mass of Great Britain is covered by roads.

The Queen has the right to any sturgeon caught off the British coast.

4 per cent of British house sellers admit to removing the house number when they leave.

Mayfair – the most expensive property on the Monopoly board – derives its name from an annual fair which was held every May until the 18th century.

12 per cent of Britons believe they have seen ghosts.

The Royal Mail uses 342 million rubber bands a year to bundle up letters.

There are some 300 fluent Cornish speakers in Britain.

4 per cent of Britons believe in the Loch Ness monster.

There are nearly 600,000 vegans in the UK.

90 per cent British households have microwaves.

Every year in Britain, some 250 people are killed or injured on motorway hard shoulders.

There are 4.2 million CCTV cameras in Britain, one for every 14 people. It's reckoned that only China and Malaysia spy more on their people than the British.

There are nearly 11 million cows in the UK.

There are 21,000 black cab taxis in London (taking 85 million fares per year, mostly in London and around Heathrow) and 40,000 minicabs.

Five million Britons have more than one job.

Some 300 languages are spoken in London, the world's most cosmopolitan city.

In the last official census, 390,000 people claimed to be Jedis – the fictional religion in *Star Wars*. This contrasts with just 250,000 Jews.

About 7 per cent of the adult UK population are vegetarians.

The oldest city in Britain is Ripon, which received its original charter in 886.

There's a village in Somerset named Curry Mallet.

Every year, the Isles of Scilly Wildlife Trust pays Prince Charles a single daffodil in rent.

The Isle of Wight and the Isle of Man have essentially the same name. 'Wight' in old English means 'man' in its wider sense of 'person'.

10 billion eggs are consumed every year in Britain.

The highest motorway in England is the M62, which goes from Liverpool to Hull.

Birds

Only 10 of the 10,000 bird species have been domesticated.

Pigeons process visual information three times quicker than we do.

Turkeys can have heart attacks.

The penguins that inhabit the tip of South America are called jackass penguins.

Puffins' feet are red in summer and yellow in winter.

It takes 42 days for an ostrich egg to hatch.

The Moa bird of New Zealand, which became extinct 400 years ago, was over 3 metres tall.

Owls have eyeballs that are tubular in shape. Because of this, they can't move their eyes, but they can rotate their heads instead.

Bald eagles build the largest nests of any bird – up to 3 metres wide and 6 metres deep.

The harpy eagle of South America feeds on monkeys.

The pheasant originated in China.

Size for size, birds live longer than mammals.

There are around 70 common breeds of chicken.

The emperor penguin can hold its breath for 20 minutes.

The ostrich has four eyelids. The inner lids are for blinking and keeping the eyeballs moist, the outer lids for attracting potential mates.

In Ireland, geese were once used to sweep chimneys. They would be pulled up chimneys by a rope tied to their legs and the beating of their wings would dislodge the soot.

On a clear day, a gobbling turkey can be heard a mile away.

The chicken is the closest living relative of tyrannosaurus rex.

An ostrich's intestinal tract is over 13 metres long.

Fossil finds show that some of the earliest bird species had four wings rather than two.

Green herons catch fish by dropping bits of bread and debris on the surface of the water as bait.

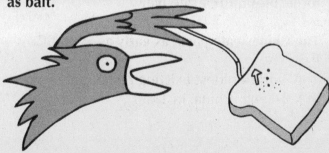

Food and drink

Rice, the main food for half the people of the world, is grown on more than 10 per cent of the earth's farmable surface.

An aubergine is a fruit (technically, a berry) as it grows on a plant and contains seeds. However, it is always treated as a vegetable.

The Brazil nut is the most naturally radioactive food.

It costs 10,000 times more to produce a litre of bottled water than a litre of tap water.

72 per cent of Britons prefer triangular sandwiches. They taste better because they encourage a small bite, releasing flavour molecules more effectively.

The Chinese ate pasta as early as 5000 BC.

The world's oldest existing restaurant opened in Kai-Feng, China, in 1153.

Every year, more than 150 million avocados are sold in the UK.

Carpaccio, the dish of thin strips of raw beef, is named after the painter Vittore Carpaccio, who used a lot of red in his paintings.

Spanish people call a plain omelette an English omelette. What we call a Spanish omelette, they call a peasant's omelette.

Lobster used to be poor people's food.

Tea is said to have been discovered in 2737 BC by a Chinese emperor when some tea leaves accidentally blew into a pot of boiling water.

Wine has been made for at least 7,000 years.

Salt is one of the few spices that is all taste and no smell.

90 per cent of the albumen (white) of an egg is made up of water.

All of an egg's vitamins A, D and E are in the yolk. Egg yolks are one of the very few foods naturally containing vitamin D.

Chop suey, Russian dressing and hamburgers all originated in the US.

Cadbury's Dairy Milk is Britain's most popular chocolate bar, with 500 million produced annually.

Adding sugar to coffee is believed to have started in 1715, in the court of King Louis XIV of France.

Ketchup was originally made from fish broth and mushrooms. Tomatoes were added later.

A 200-year-old piece of Tibetan cheese was auctioned off for $1,513 in 1993.

Last year, we Britons drank 6 billion cups of tea.

Cornish pasties – pies containing meat, potato, swede and onion – were given a thick, fluted sealing edge to make them easier for tin miners to hold with dirty hands.

History

When the railway was invented, some people believed that anyone travelling faster than 12 mph risked mental problems.

King Henry III kept a quartet of lions in the Tower of London.

In 1837 the Russian author Alexander Pushkin was killed in a duel.

Queen Anne (1702–1714) banned the wearing of spectacles, inappropriate wigs and the smoking of pipes in St James's Palace.

Queen Victoria had hot water and clothes sent to Prince Albert's room every morning for years after his death.

A man attempted to assassinate Queen Mary I (1553–1558) by climbing St James's Palace and using a large lens to focus the sun's rays on her while she was walking below. It failed.

The Anglo-Saxons believed Friday to be such an unlucky day that they ritually slaughtered any child unfortunate enough to be born on that day.

In 1837 Queen Victoria became the first monarch to live in Buckingham Palace.

In the 17th century the Great Hall at Westminster Palace was used as a shopping precinct.

The Russian composer Tchaikovsky was financed by a wealthy widow for 13 years. At her request, they never met.

Cleopatra married Ptolemy XIII and then, when he died, she married his brother, Ptolemy XIV.

At the age of 88, Michelangelo was still sculpting.

In the Second World War, Chrysler built the B-29s that bombed Japan; Mitsubishi built the Zeros that tried to shoot them down. The two companies now build cars together.

Sir Isaac Newton was an ordained priest in the Church of England.

After the French Revolution of 1789, selling sour, below-standard wine was considered against the national interest and the merchants doing so were executed.

QUALITY VINO! (HONEST)

Sutoku, an emperor of Japan, copied out the Lankauru Sutra, a 10,500-word Buddhist tract, in his own blood.

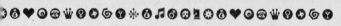
Vikings used the skulls of their enemies as drinking vessels.

Queen Elizabeth I wasn't buried until five weeks after her death.

The great Gothic cathedral of Milan was started in 1386 but only completed in 1805.

Mary Stuart became Queen of Scotland when she was only six days old.

During the American revolution, many brides wore the colour red instead of white as a symbol of rebellion.

Before the Second World War, it was sacrilege to touch an emperor of Japan.

Queen Anne is said to have died from a fit of apoplexy, due to overeating, while at an outdoor supper party at Kensington Palace in 1714.

Human beings

A human being can taste one gram of salt in 500 litres of water.

The average person will spend some six months of his or her life on the toilet.

The common cold will delay a child's growth for the duration of the cold.

In terms of mortality, the safest age is 10 years old.

Apparently, the most relaxing image you can imagine is rain falling at a slant.

The hand with the larger and squarer thumbnail is likely to be your dominant hand.

A quarter of all children have one or more sleepwalking episodes before the age of 12.

22 per cent of twins are left-handed. In the non-twin population, the number is just under 10 per cent.

Too much vitamin A can kill you.

The colour green is said to be effective in relieving homesickness.

The average human eye can distinguish about 500 different shades of grey.

The more wrinkles your brain has, the more intelligent you are.

The period between the hours of four and six in the afternoon is when people are the most irritable.

Drinking a glass of water after eating reduces the acid in your mouth by more than 60 per cent.

While we're resting, the air we breathe passes through our noses at four miles per hour.

Every hour we breathe over 1,500 litres of air.

The loss of just 15 per cent of the body's water can be fatal.

Brainwave activity in humans changes when we catch the punch line of a joke.

While reading a page of print, our eyes don't move continuously across the page. Instead, they move in a series of jumps, called 'fixations', from one clump of words to the next.

Whispering is more wearing on your voice than a normal speaking tone. Whispering and shouting stretch the vocal cords.

We can live four times as long without food than we can without water.

Constant exercising can be just as bad for a person as no exercise at all. The human body needs 24 hours without exercise about once a week to cleanse itself of lactic acid and other waste products.

On an average day, an adult spends 77 minutes eating.

The sound of a snore can be almost as loud as the noise of a pneumatic drill.

Within the first hour of birth, a baby is able to recognize its mother's smell.

You can guess what sex someone is with 95 per cent accuracy just by smelling their breath.

The average cough comes out of your mouth at 60 miles per hour.

If one identical twin grows up without a certain tooth coming in, the second identical twin will usually also grow up without the tooth.

Reptiles

Reptiles are never slimy. Their scales have few glands, and are usually silky to the touch.

For most snakes, breathing is accomplished with just one lung.

Basilisks are sometimes called Jesus Christ lizards because of their ability to run on water.

If you are chased by a crocodile, run zigzag, as a crocodile isn't good at making sharp turns.

The mountain devil, a lizard-like creature native to Australia, never drinks: it absorbs tiny drops of dew through its skin.

The gastric juices of a snake can digest bones and teeth – but not fur or hair.

Snakes don't bite in rivers or swamps because they would drown if they did.

Many reptiles can replace limbs or tails if they're lost or damaged but only the aquatic newt has the ability to regenerate the lens of its eye.

The chameleon releases its tongue at 26 body lengths per second – faster than the human eye can see. It hits its prey in about 0.03 seconds.

The gaboon viper is the world's most poisonous snake.

Milk snakes lay about 13 eggs – in piles of animal manure.

Tiger snakes can survive perfectly well when

their eyes are pecked out by seagulls.

The length of any alligator is 12 times the distance between its eyes.

The tuatara's metabolism is so slow it only has to breathe once an hour.

Science

The reason bubbles are round is because this is the most efficient shape that soap film can take to accommodate the air trapped inside.

Just one litre of used motor oil can ruin one million litres of fresh water.

The strength of early lasers was measured in Gillettes – the number of razor blades a beam could puncture.

You could walk on custard, if you wanted, because it will get thick when pressure is applied to it.

Fires usually move faster uphill than downhill.

Helium is the element with the lowest boiling point.

Atoms are so tiny that there are more atoms in a single grain of sand than there are grains of sand on a beach.

Nine out of every ten scientists who ever lived are alive today.

The earliest type of robot was a water clock invented in Egypt in 250 BC.

<----> >----< is the Muller-Lyer illusion. Despite what you might think, both lines are of the same length.

There are sweeteners that are about 200,000 times sweeter than sugar.

You've heard the expression 'a hair's breadth', as in, for example, 'the two runners were neck and neck: never more than a hair's breadth apart'. Well, a hair's breadth is actually 0.05cm (a.k.a. half a millimetre).

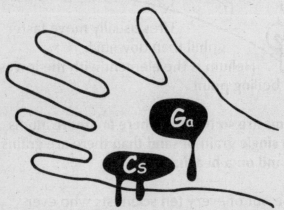

Cesium and gallium are both metals that would melt in your hand, as they are exposed to your body temperature.

If hot water is poured into a glass, that glass is more likely to break if it is thick than if it is thin. This is why test tubes are made of thin glass.

Sea life

Squid have three hearts and ten tentacles.

A giant clam has 35 eyes and they're all blue.

One in 5,000 north Atlantic lobsters are born bright blue.

More than 20 million seahorses are harvested each year for folk medicinal purposes. The world seahorse population has dropped 70 per cent in the past 10 years.

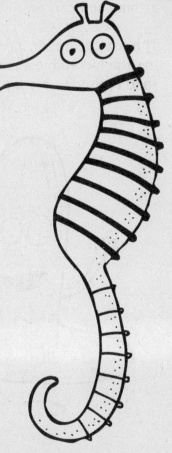

If they get very upset, octopuses can eat themselves.

Sea sponges are used in drugs for treating asthma and cancer.

The sea cucumber, a relative of the starfish, has the incredible ability to change from solid to fluid to escape predators.

The way we live

Percentage of men who wash their hands after using the toilet: 55 per cent.

Percentage of women who wash their hands after using a toilet: 80 per cent.

Most people button their shirts upwards.

Children between the ages of two and seven spend an average of 28 minutes a day colouring in.

45 per cent of Britons reckon they don't get enough sleep.

55 per cent of British workers say they never take a lunch break.

At any given time, about 0.7 per cent of the world's population is drunk.

29 per cent of British women cut the size labels off their clothes.

12 per cent of married British men claim to do most of the housework. (The rest tell the truth!)

For every mile travelled, death is 140 times more likely in a car than in a plane. However, cars are safer than planes on a per journey basis.

Only 29 per cent of British families sit down to eat a meal together more than once a week.

The space spanning 1.2 metres from the sides of parked cars is known to cyclists as 'the door zone'.

We tend to stand 35cm apart when we talk to each other.

Brushing your teeth with the tap on wastes about 20 litres of water.

Only 7 per cent of British people say they trust their neighbours.

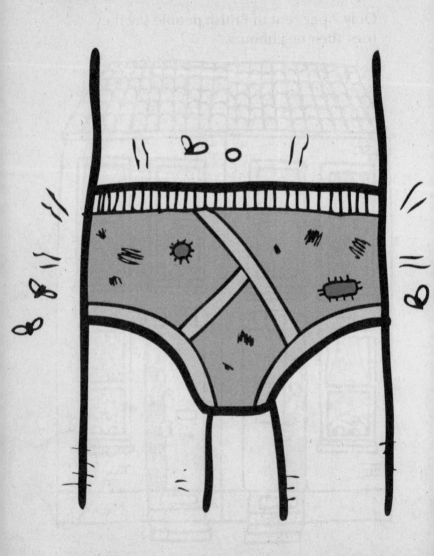

10 per cent of British adults admit to wearing the same item of underwear three days in a row.

If the entire population of earth was reduced to exactly 100 people, 50 per cent of the world's currency would be held by six of them.

4 per cent of the food you eat will be eaten in front of the fridge with its door open.

The average Briton spends more than 400 hours a year shopping.

It is estimated that 60 per cent of smoke detectors do not work, either because they don't have batteries in them or because the batteries are dead.

A quarter of British adults have no savings at all.

The average person opens the fridge 22 times a day.

Dentists recommend that a toothbrush be

kept at least two metres away from a toilet to avoid airborne particles resulting from the flush.

23 per cent of the UK population live in the countryside.

86 per cent of women and 72 per cent of men look at price tags when they shop.

68 per cent of Britons say they believe in the existence of ghosts and/or spirits.

The average Briton spends two hours and 44 minutes a day on the internet.

The average person keeps magazines for 29 weeks before throwing them out.

Men are almost twice as likely as women to take a day off work claiming to have flu.

The average person throws away seven times their body weight in rubbish every year.

Eight million nappies are thrown away in the UK every day.

In a typical restaurant, customers receive 27 pence worth of food for every pound they spend.

The average Briton drinks 33 litres of bottled water a year.

50 years ago, 90 per cent of British adults owned a Bible; today fewer than two-thirds do.

An office chair with wheels will travel about $7\frac{1}{2}$ miles a year.

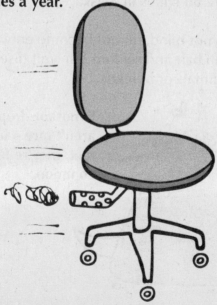

Things that are not what they seem or what you thought

Banana oil doesn't come from bananas: it's made from petroleum.

Handling frogs doesn't cause warts.

The Vikings never wore horned helmets.

There are no igloos in Alaska.

Bats are not blind, do not become entangled in human hair and seldom transmit disease to other animals or humans.

Dinosaur droppings aren't rare – in fact, they're fairly common.

Animals

The night monkey of Central America rarely ventures out during daylight as its unusual golden eyes see best in the dark.

The most money ever paid for a cow in an auction was $1.3 million.

Sheep self-medicate by grazing on herbs when they have a stomach ailment.

An elephant can eat a quarter of a ton of grass in a day.

When an armadillo is frightened it jumps straight into the air.

Cats can suffer from 258 different genetic diseases.

An armadillo can walk under water.

To enable it to pull its body into a tight, prickly ball for defence, the hedgehog has a large muscle running along its stomach.

A baby beaver stays with its parents for two years.

There's a blue sheep. The bharal or the Himalayan blue sheep has a coat with a slight blue sheen.

A cat year is equivalent to about five human years.

Elephant herds post their own sentries. When danger threatens, the sentry raises its trunk and the rest of the herd is alerted.

Domestic cats kill more than 57 million creatures a year in the UK – over half of which are birds.

The oldest known horse in the world lived to be 62.

Greatest Britons of all time?

These were the winners in a 2002 poll.

1. Sir Winston Churchill (with 27.9 per cent of the total vote)

2. Isambard Kingdom Brunel (24.1 per cent)

3. Diana, Princess of Wales (14.2 per cent)

4. Charles Darwin (6.9 per cent)

5. William Shakespeare (6.9 per cent)

6. Sir Isaac Newton (5.2 per cent)

7. Queen Elizabeth I (4.5 per cent)

8. John Lennon (4.3 per cent)

9. Admiral Lord Nelson (3.1 per cent)

10. Oliver Cromwell (2.9 per cent)

Creepy crawlies

All spiders are carnivorous – that's to say,
meat-eating. They're also cannibals and will
eat other spiders. Their usual diet is flies. A
large fly can take 12 hours to consume.

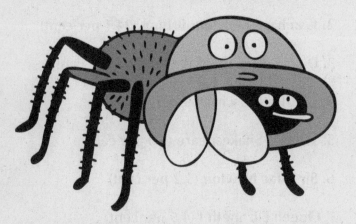

Female earwigs can't distinguish their own
eggs from those of other earwigs, and so tend
to any they find.

There are some 18,000 species of butterfly.

The aphid's reproductive cycle is so fast that
females are born pregnant.

Cockroaches break wind every 15 minutes. Even after they die, they carry on releasing methane gas for another 18 hours.

Most snails are hermaphrodites, meaning they have both female and male reproductive organs.

The colour a head louse will be as an adult depends on the colour of the person's hair in which it 'lives'.

Ants evolved from wasps more than 100 million years ago.

Some species of snail are poisonous. Their venom can be fatal to humans.

Dracula ants are so-called because they suck the blood of their young.

The jaw of the trap-jaw ant snaps shut 2,000 times faster than the blink of an eye.

Most butterflies fly by day while most moths fly by night.

The water spider, which lives underwater, uses special hairs to trap air around its body and allow it to breathe.

A 13-year-old boy in India produced winged beetles in his urine after hatching the eggs in his body.

Spiders liquefy their prey before consuming it.

First 10 men in space

Yuri Gagarin (USSR)

Alan B. Shepard (USA)

Virgil ('Gus') Grissom (USA)

Gherman Titov (USSR)

John Glenn (USA)

Malcolm Scott Carpenter (USA)

Andrian Nikolayev (USSR)

Pavel Popovich (USSR)

Walter Schirra (USA)

Leroy Gordon Cooper (USA)

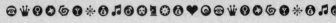
Einstein

Albert Einstein (1879–1955) is widely accepted as the greatest scientist of the 20th century – and maybe of all time. However, he was an unusual man.

As I've written in previous books, he couldn't speak properly until he was nine.

He was once offered the presidency of Israel but declined, saying he had no head for problems.

He failed his first college entrance exam.

He never learned to drive.

He was awarded the 1921 Nobel Prize for Physics.

Towards the end of his life he became a vegetarian.

He had a chemical element – einsteinium – named after him.

When he was inducted as an American citizen, he attended the ceremony without socks.

When he died, his final words died with him – the nurse at his side didn't understand German.

In 1999 the influential American magazine *Time* named him 'Person of the Century'.

London Zoo's stars from the past

Obaysch the Hippopotamus, who arrived at the zoo in 1850, was the first hippo seen in Europe since the Roman Empire, and the first in England since prehistory.

Jumbo the Elephant, who arrived at the zoo in 1865, subsequently gave his name to anything large in size. He became aggressive in old age and was sold to Phineas Barnum's circus. He died after being hit by a train.

Winnie the American Black Bear, given to the zoo in 1914, inspired A. A. Milne to write the Winnie-the-Pooh books. A. A. Milne used to visit the zoo with his son, Christopher Robin.

Josephine the Great Indian Hornbill was for many years the oldest animal at the zoo. She lived in the Bird House until her death in 1998 aged 53.

Guy the Gorilla lived at the zoo from 1947

until his death in 1978, and was so loved by visitors that he is commemorated in a statue.

Brumas, born in 1949, was the first polar bear to be born at London Zoo. Thought to be a male, it later transpired she was female. In 1950, because of her, the zoo's attendance figures for the year hit the 3 million mark (1 million more than usual). This figure hasn't been exceeded since.

Chi Chi was the zoo's first giant panda. She arrived in 1958.

Goldie the Golden Eagle became a national celebrity when he escaped for two weeks in 1965 and flew around the roads and trees of Regent's Park.

Things said about zoos

'Zoo: An excellent place to study the habits of human beings.' (Evan Esar)

'When I was a kid I said to my father one afternoon, "Will you take me to the zoo?" He answered, "If the zoo wants you, let them come and get you."' (Jerry Lewis)

'My parents used to take me to the pet department and tell me it was a zoo.' (Billy Connolly)

'I've actually gone to the zoo and had monkeys shout to me from their cages, "I'm in here, when you're walking around like that?"' (Robin Williams)

What a 10-stone (64kg) person would weigh elsewhere in our solar system

Pluto – 3.18kg

Moon – 10.91kg

Mercury – 24.09kg

Mars – 24.09kg

Uranus – 57.73kg

Venus – 62.27kg

Saturn – 68.64kg

Neptune – 75.45kg

Jupiter – 161.36kg

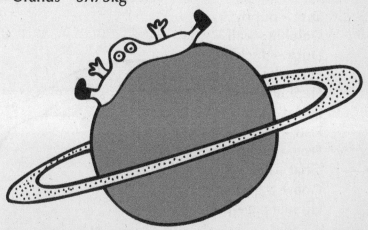

The names we give to baby creatures

Ant – antling
Alligator – hatchling
Badger – cub
Barn owl – owlet
Beaver – kit, kitten
      or pup
Bird – chick
Cat – kitten
Chicken – chick
Cow – calf
Deer – fawn

Dog – puppy
Dolphin – calf
Duck – duckling
Eel – elver
Elephant – calf
Ferret – kit
Fish – fry
Frog – tadpole or froglet
Goat – kid
Goose – gosling
Guinea pig – pup

Hare – leveret
Hippopotamus – calf
Hedgehog – hoglet
Horse – foal
Kangaroo – joey
Koala – joey
Otter – cub
Pig – piglet
Pigeon – squab
Rabbit – kitten
Rat – pup
Seal – pup

Sheep – lamb
Spider – spiderling
Swan – cygnet
Toad – tadpole
Tortoise – hatchling
Wolf – cub
Zebra – foal

Words

If you try to say the alphabet without moving your lips or your tongue, every letter will sound exactly the same.

According to linguistics experts, the easiest sounds for the human ear to hear are (in order): 'ah', 'aw', 'eh' and 'oo'.

Nine words – the, of, and, to, it, you, be, have, will – make up a quarter of all the words used in English.

Fickleheaded and *fiddledeedee* are the longest English words in the dictionary that only use the letters in the first half of the alphabet.

Polish is the only word in the English language that when capitalized is changed from a noun or a verb to a nationality.

'Accommodate' is the most misspelled word in English.

The Lord's Prayer contains just 68 words.

The word *karaoke* means 'empty orchestra' in Japanese.

If you take away a letter from the word 'startling', you'll form a new word every time: startling, starting, staring, string, sting, sing, sin, in, I.

'Fraternity' used to be a term applied by groups of thieves to themselves.

Adding just one letter to the middle of the one-syllable world 'smile' turns it into the three-syllable word 'simile'.

The longest words with vertical symmetry (the left half is a mirror image of the right half) are OTTO, MA'AM and TOOT.

The word 'infant' comes from the Latin words meaning 'not speaking'.

The word 'salary' is derived from the word 'salt'. In Roman times, salt was often used instead of money.

There's no word for 'weather' in the Hawaiian language – presumably because the weather there is always so fine.

No Hawaiian word ends in a consonant.

The words 'polysyllabic', 'fifteen-lettered' and 'unhyphenated' are all autological, in that they describe themselves. So 'polysyllabic' – meaning having many syllables – has many syllables. Similarly, the word 'fifteen-lettered' has 15 letters and 'unhyphenated' is indeed unhyphenated!

Here is a word that looks the same whether written all in capitals – COUSCOUS – or all in lower case – couscous.

The Old English word for 'sneeze' is *fneosam*.

fneosam

'Strengthlessnesses', 18 letters long, is the longest word in the English language with just one (repeated) vowel.

German is considered the sister language of English.

The word 'hobnob' comes from two Old English words, *habban* ('to have') and *nabban* ('to have not'). 'Hobnob' was used to describe the practice of buying drinks in turns: it meant having to buy a round and not having to buy a round.

The Mayans have a word, *huuyub*, meaning 'to draw breath with a puckered mouth after eating chillies'.

When George Bernard Shaw was asked if he knew that 'sugar' was the only word in the English language where 'su' was pronounced 'sh', he replied, 'Sure.' Think about it!

The alphabet in order of most common use (based on *The Oxford English Dictionary*) goes: E A R I O T N S L C U D P M H G B F Y W K V X Z J Q.

Written by pupils in English essays

The plan was simple, like my brother Phil. But unlike Phil, this plan just might work.

The young fighter had a hungry look, the kind you get from not eating for a while.

His thoughts tumbled in his head, making and breaking alliances like underpants in a tumble dryer.

Her hair glistened in the rain like nose hair after a sneeze.

The little boat gently drifted across the pond exactly the way a bowling ball wouldn't.

Her eyes were like two brown circles with big black dots in the centre.

Her vocabulary was as bad as, like, whatever.

He was as tall as a six-foot-three-inch tree.

The politician was gone but unnoticed, like the full stop after the Dr on a Dr Pepper can.

John and Mary had never met. They were like two hummingbirds who had also never met.

The thunder was ominous-sounding, much like the sound of a thin sheet of metal being shaken backstage during the storm scene in a play.

The red-brick wall was the colour of a brick-red crayon.

Her artistic sense was exquisitely refined, like someone who can tell butter from 'I Can't Believe It's Not Butter'.

She had a deep, throaty, genuine laugh, like that sound a dog makes just before it throws up.

She walked into my office like a centipede
with 98 missing legs.

It hurt the way your tongue hurts after you
accidentally staple it to the wall.

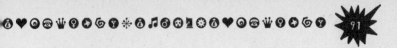
Beards

A blond beard grows faster than any other colour hair.

The horror writer Stephen King usually wears a beard between October and February.

The composer Frédéric Chopin wore a beard on the left side of his face. 'It does not matter: my audience sees only my right side.'

Beards are the fastest-growing hairs on the human body. If a man never trimmed his beard, it would grow to over 9 metres in his lifetime.

If an Amish man has a beard, he's married.

In early 16th-century England, men would often keep their tooth pick in their beards.

However, Queen Elizabeth I disliked beards and so put a tax on them. Perhaps Good Queen Bess had a fear of beards? If so, she was suffering from pogonophobia.

The only member of the rock band ZZ Top not to wear a full beard is the drummer, whose name is . . . Frank Beard.

There are many types of beard. Here are just some of them: Forked, Needle, Bodkin, Ducktail, Breakwater, Cathedral, Goatee, Old Dutch, Anchor, Vandyke.

Celebrity anagrams

GEM POSING Simon Pegg

NOW COME ILLS Simon Cowell

RANDOM ADVICE David Cameron

FOOT ENTRANCE Fearne Cotton

MEN HELP HUNTERS Stephen Mulhern

ARAB CAB AMOK Barack Obama

NOW EASE ILL Leona Lewis

TURNED STINKS Kirsten Dunst

BURN LESS LARD Russell Brand

REPLY PLAIN HIP Ryan Phillippe

ANY RUM YARD Andy Murray

FARM PARKLAND Frank Lampard

NO KNAVERY Vernon Kay

RAVAGES NOWHERE Owen Hargreaves

Things you can order in an American diner . . .

And what you will get:

Belch water – a glass of seltzer or soda water.

Adam and Eve on a raft – two poached eggs on toast.

Bowl of red – a serving of chilli.

Cowboy with spurs – an omelette with chips.

Eve with the lid on – apple pie.

Nervous pudding – jelly.

Put out the lights and cry – liver with onions.

Brown cow – chocolate milk.

Wreck a pair – two scrambled eggs.

Words invented by Shakespeare

The Oxford English Dictionary (OED) has verified that Shakespeare originated the following words (amongst many others) or, more likely, was the first to use them in print.

Aerial

Amazement

Arch-villain

Bedazzle

Bloodsucking

Colourful

Fairyland

Fortune-teller

Grovel

Leaky

Leapfrog

Lonely

Puke

Rant

Schoolboy

Shipwrecked

Shooting star

Squabble

Zany

Celebrities and what their mothers do/did for a living

Kanye West – University professor.

Lily Allen – Film producer.

Coleen McLoughlin – Nursery nurse.

Zac Efron – Secretary.

James McAvoy – Psychiatric nurse.

Orlando Bloom – Teacher.

Simon Cowell – Ballet dancer.

Leona Lewis – Social worker.

Shia LaBeouf – Ballerina.

Hilary Duff – Music producer.

Christian Slater – Casting director.

**Wayne Rooney – Part-time cleaner at the
school Coleen McLoughlin attended.**

Wayne Rooney – Part-time cleaner at the school Coleen McLoughlin attended.

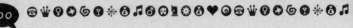

Birds

The swan has the most feathers of any bird.

Dimorphic egrets wave one of their bright yellow feet over the water to attract possible food to the surface.

At 24 billion, there are more chickens in the world than any other bird.

The male cockerel makes noises pretending that he's found food as a way of luring (female) hens.

Birds don't have sweat glands, so their bodies cool down by flight or, when at rest, by panting.

The broad-tailed hummingbird drinks five times its own body weight in nectar every day.

In Japan, carrion crows have discovered a brilliant way to get walnuts out of their shells. They wait until cars stop at traffic lights, then

they fly down and place walnuts in front of
the tyres. When the lights change, the cars
run over the nuts and crack them.

**Parrots have the largest brains in relation to
body size of any bird.**

The raven tricks its rival into
thinking there's food
elsewhere and then
sneaks back to eat
what it wanted in
the first place.

**The frigate
bird can fly
at a speed of
260 mph.**

The most
populous bird species
is the red-billed quelea
of southern Africa. There are an
estimated 100 trillion of them.

**Turkeys will peck to death members of the
flock that are physically inferior or different.**

Mallee fowl chicks are born buried alive and have to burrow their way out of the sand.

Parrots have much better hearing than humans. During the First World War, the French kept parrots on the top of the Eiffel Tower to warn of the approach of German planes.

A parrot can shut its beak with a force of up to 60kg per square centimetre.

Birds don't sleep in their nests, though they may rest in them from time to time.

Emperor penguins will sometimes kidnap baby penguins.

Birds have the ability to change the level of their birdsong if they have to overcome the sound of traffic or other urban noise.

People who got dogs from Battersea Dogs' Home

Simon Callow
Geri Halliwell
Sir Elton John
Kevin Spacey
Ringo Starr
Jack Davenport

Singular Oscar achievements

The only film with an all-Indian cast to win the Best Picture Oscar is *Slumdog Millionaire* in 2009.

The only role to be nominated for an Oscar twice in the same year is Queen Elizabeth I (in 1999, Cate Blanchett was nominated for playing her in *Elizabeth* while Dame Judi Dench was nominated for playing her in *Shakespeare In Love*.

The only daughter of a Best Actor winner to win an Oscar for Best Supporting Actress was Angelina Jolie for *Girl Interrupted* (2000). She is the daughter of Jon Voight, who won for *Coming Home* (1979).

The only films to win Oscars in every category for which they were nominated: *Lord of The Rings*: *The Return of The King* (11/11 Oscars in 2004); *The Last Emperor* (9/9 in 1988) and *Gigi* (9/9 in 1959).

The only Oscar to win an Oscar: Oscar Hammerstein II (Best Song: 1941 & 1945).

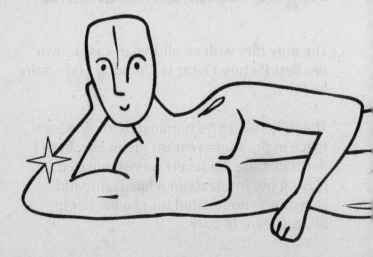

The only actress to win an Oscar for playing an Oscar nominee: Maggie Smith in *California Suite* (1978).

The only person to open the Oscar envelope and find their own name on the card: Irving Berlin (Best Song, 'White Christmas' 1942).

The only two actors to tie for Best Actor: Wallace Beery, *The Champ* and Fredric March, *Dr Jekyll And Mr Hyde* (1931/32).

The only two actresses to tie for Best Actress: Katharine Hepburn, *The Lion in Winter,* and Barbra Streisand, *Funny Girl* (1968).

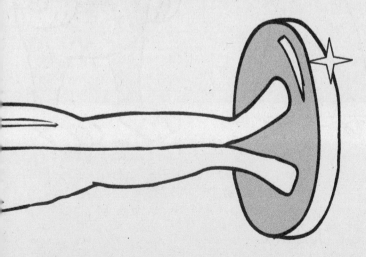

The only actresses to win Best Actress Oscars for their very first on-screen appearances: Shirley Booth (*Come Back Little Sheba*, 1953), Julie Andrews (*Mary Poppins*, 1965), Barbra Streisand (*Funny Girl*, 1969), Marlee Matlin (*Children of A Lesser God*, 1987).

The only actress to win an Oscar for just eight minutes' work: Dame Judi Dench, in *Shakespeare in Love* (1998).

The only animation film nominated for Best Film: *Beauty and the Beast* (1991).

The only actors to win consecutive Oscars: Spencer Tracy (1937 and 1938), Jason Robards (1976 and 1977) and Tom Hanks (1993 and 1994).

The only actresses to win consecutive Oscars: Luise Rainer (1936 and 1937) and Katharine Hepburn (1967 and 1968).

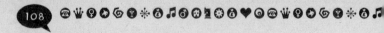

History

The Roman Emperor Caligula made his horse a senator.

The Krakatoa volcano eruption of 1883 resulted in the deaths of more than 36,000 people. It was so powerful it was heard 3,000 miles away. The moon shone blue for two years afterwards.

King James I introduced a swear box to St James's Palace, and all the money was given to the poor.

Throughout history, the most destructive disease has been malaria. More than 1.5 million people die from malaria every year.

During the First Crusade there was a band of religious hysterics who marched behind a goose they believed was filled with the Holy Spirit.

King Charles II was a keen tennis player and would weigh himself before and after every

game to see how much weight he had lost during it.

Cleopatra tested her poisons by giving them to her slaves.

from: Cleopatra X

The Circus Maximus in Rome could hold up to 250,000 people. An equal number could view the games from the adjoining hills.

The 16th-century Escorial palace of King Phillip II of Spain had 1,200 doors.

King George III said he didn't like Hampton Court because when he was a boy, his grandfather used to box his ears there.

Napoleon Bonaparte finished bottom of his class at military school.

A 17th-century Swedish philologist (an academic who studies languages) claimed that in the Garden of Eden, God spoke Swedish, Adam spoke Danish and the serpent spoke French.

In Puritan times, to be born on a Sunday was interpreted as a sign of great sin.

The Spanish Inquisition condemned the entire country of the Netherlands to death for heresy.

There were 57 countries involved in the Second World War.

The longest surviving veteran of the American War of Independence (1775–1783) was Daniel F. Bakeman, who died in 1869 at the age of 109.

Queen Victoria banned the colour black from her funeral and left instructions for her mourners to wear white.

King Charles I's dog accompanied him to his execution.

During the 15th century, sick people were often dressed in red and surrounded by red objects because it was believed the colour red would help them to get better.

Benjamin Franklin's peers decided not to give him the task of writing the Declaration of Independence because they feared he would conceal a joke in it.

More than 100 descendants of the composer Johann Sebastian Bach have been cathedral organists.

IN CONGRESS

What did Benjamin Franklin say when he discovered electricity?

I'm deeply shocked

Tsar Paul I of Russia banished soldiers to Siberia for marching out of step.

Queen Isabella of Castile, who sponsored Christopher Columbus in his travels, boasted that she had only had two baths in her life – at her birth and before she got married.

Names famous people

PERSON	PET
Russell Brand	Cat
Jim Carrey	Iguana
Venus Williams	Dog
Paris Hilton	Dog (Chihuahua)
Miley Ray Cyrus	Dogs
Fearne Cotton	Cats
Anthony Horowitz	Dog (Labrador)
Zac Efron	Dogs
Ashley Tisdale	Siamese cat
Kate Bosworth	Dog
Jake Gyllenhaal	Cats
Angelina Jolie	Dog
Paul O'Grady	Rat
Julia Roberts	Dog
Princess Beatrice	Dog
Prince William	Dog (Terrier)
Snoop Dog	Dog (Pitbull)
Davina McCall	Dog
Madonna	Dog
Jessica Simpson	Pig
Cameron Diaz	Cat
Sara Cox	Dog (Basset Hound)

gave to their pets

NAME

Morrissey
Houston
Pete (named after Pete Sampras)
Tinkerbell
Loco, Juicy and Minnie Pearl
Tallulah and Keloy
Lucky
Dreamer and Puppy
Simon
Maui
Louise and Dusty
Atticus
Harry
Buster
Gatsby
Wat
Dirty Red
Chloe
Pepito
Brutus
The Little Man
Snoop (after Snoop Doggy Dog)

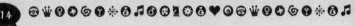
Things said about pets

'Animals are such agreeable friends – they ask no questions, they pass no criticisms.' (George Eliot)

'You can say any fool thing to a dog, and the dog will give you this look that says, "My God, you're RIGHT! I NEVER would've thought of that!"' (Dave Barry)

'Our perfect companions never have fewer than four feet.' (Colette)

'A dog is the only thing on earth that loves you more than he loves himself.' (Josh Billings)

'He who is cruel to animals becomes hard also in his dealings with men. We can judge the heart of a man by his treatment of animals.' (Immanuel Kant)

'I have been studying the traits and dispositions of the "lower animals" (so called) and contrasting them with the traits

and dispositions of man. I find the result humiliating to me.' (Mark Twain)

'There is no psychiatrist in the world like a puppy licking your face.' (Ben Williams)

'If dogs could talk, perhaps we would find it as hard to get along with them as we do with people.' (Josef Capek)

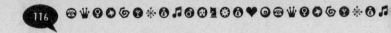

The Bible

Psalms 117 is the centre chapter in the Bible.

Salt is mentioned more than 30 times in the Bible.

The two animals referred to most frequently in the Bible are sheep/lamb and lion in that order.

Pigs are mentioned just twice in the Bible.

There is no mention of rats in the Bible.

The longest verse in the Bible is Esther 8:9.

There are more than 1,700 references to gems and precious stones in the Bible.

At 18 letters, Mahershalalhashbaz (Isaiah 18:1) is the longest word in the Bible.

There are 929 chapters in the Old Testament, containing 592,439 words.

There are 260 chapters in the New Testament, containing 181,253 words.
It is believed that Shakespeare was 46 around the time the King James Version of the Bible was written. In Psalms 46, the 46th word is shake and the 46th word from the end is spear.

The Bible has been translated into Klingon.

Some biblical scholars believe that Aramaic (the language of the ancient Bible) did not contain an easy way to say 'many things' and used a term that has come down to us as forty. This means that when the Bible – in many places – refers to 'forty days', it simply means many days.

The 'chapters' of the New Testament were not there originally. When monks in medieval times translated it from the Greek, they numbered the chapters in each 'book'.

Only children

Shia LaBeouf
Dale Winton
Sir Elton John
Robert De Niro
Charlotte Church
Chris Tarrant
Sir Anthony Hopkins

Pure trivia

The American poet Emily Dickinson wrote more than 900 poems but only four were published in her lifetime.

The American games Advance to Boardwalk, Free Parking and Don't Go to Jail are all spin-offs from the game of Monopoly.

It's forbidden to take photographs at a Quaker wedding.

Children in the Chinook Indian tribe used to be strapped between boards from head to toe

so they would have fashionably flat skulls.

In the 16th century, a Turkish woman could divorce her husband if he failed to keep his family's pot filled with coffee.

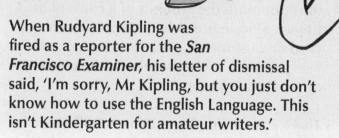

In 1938 Phyllis Newcombe, 22, combusted spontaneously at a dance hall during a waltz.

When Rudyard Kipling was fired as a reporter for the *San Francisco Examiner*, his letter of dismissal said, 'I'm sorry, Mr Kipling, but you just don't know how to use the English Language. This isn't Kindergarten for amateur writers.'

The nursery rhyme 'Who Killed Cock Robin' refers to the death of the legendary Robin Hood.

The French critic Sainte Beuve was involved

in a duel. When asked to choose his weapons, he replied, 'I choose spelling. You're dead.'

In order for a deck of cards to be mixed up properly, it should be shuffled seven times.

6 is a perfect number. The numbers that go into 6 – 1, 2 and 3 – add up to 6.

The loudest sound that could be made in 1600 was on a pipe organ.

A nun tried unsuccessfully to grow mushrooms in the grounds of a convent in Clwyd. Since her death in 1986, a decent crop of mushrooms has grown on her grave every autumn. Nowhere else in the convent do mushrooms grow.

There is no living descendant of William Shakespeare.

Pokémon stands for pocket monster.

Head boys and girls at school

Matt Smith (Northampton School for Boys)
Prince Edward (Gordonstoun)
Boris Johnson (Eton)
Sir Ian McKellen (Bolton)
Sarah, Duchess of York (Hurst Lodge)
Kate Winslet (Redroofs Theatre School)
J. K. Rowling (Wyedean Comprehensive in
   Chepstow)

Animals

Elephants communicate in sound waves
below the frequency humans can hear.

**A lion in the wild usually makes no more than
20 kills a year.**

A pair of mice can produce 500 offspring in a
year.

**A jackrabbit can travel more than 3.6 metres
in one bound.**

The male fox will mate for life, and if the female dies, he remains single. However, if the male dies, the female will hook up with a new mate.

Cows produce 20 per cent of all methane released into the atmosphere.

Chimps can be taught to understand the different values of numbers and remember them years later.

The falabella is the world's smallest breed of horse.

Male marmoset monkeys put on weight in sympathy with their pregnant mates.

You can tell the sex of a horse by its teeth. Most males have 40; females have 36.

Rabbits are more closely related to horses than they are to rodents or mice.

An extinct species of kangaroo had a head the size of a Shetland pony's and reached a height of more than 3 metres.

Beavers were once the size of bears.

Rats multiply so quickly that in 18 months, two rats could have over a million descendants.

Elephants and chimps have around 30 different sounds to communicate things to one another. By comparison, horses have six.

Written by pupils in history essays

In midevil times most people were alliterate.

Julius Caesar extinguished himself on the battlefields of Gaul. The Ides of March murdered him because they thought he was going to be made king. Dying, he gasped out: 'Tee hee, Brutus.'

The Bible is full of interesting caricatures. In the first book of the Bible, Guinessis, Adam and Eve were created from an apple tree.

One of their children, Cain, asked, 'Am I my brother's son?'

Socrates was a famous Greek teacher who went around giving people advice. They killed him. Socrates died from an overdose of wedlock. After his death, his career suffered a dramatic decline.

In the Olympic games, Greeks ran races, jumped, hurled the biscuits and threw the java.

Moses led the Hebrew slaves to the Red Sea, where they made unleavened bread, which is bread made without any ingredients. Moses went up on Mount Cyanide to get the ten commandments. He died before he ever reached Canada.

Ancient Egypt was inhabited by mummies and they all wrote in hydraulics. They lived in the Sarah Dessert and traveled by Camelot. The climate of the Sarah is such that the inhabitants have to live elsewhere.

Finally Magna Carta provided that no man should be hanged twice for the same offense.

Another story was William Tell, who shot an arrow through an apple while standing on his son's head.

Eventually, the Romans conquered the Greeks. History calls people Romans because they never stayed in one place for very long.

Abraham Lincoln became America's greatest Precedent. Lincoln's mother died in infancy, and he was born in a log cabin which he built with his own hands. Abraham Lincoln freed the slaves by signing the Emasculation Proclamation. On the night of April 14, 1865, Lincoln went to the theatre and got shot in his seat by one of the actors in a moving picture show. The believed assinator was John Wilkes Booth, a supposingly insane actor. This ruined Booth's career.

Bach was the most famous composer in the world and so was Handel. Handel was half German, half Italian and half English. He was very large.

The sun never set on the British Empire because the British Empire is in the East and the sun sets in the West. Queen Victoria was the longest queen. She sat on a thorn for 63 years. She was a moral woman who practised virtue. Her death was the final event which ended her reign.

Beethoven wrote music even though he was deaf. He was so deaf he wrote loud music. He took long walks in the forest even when everyone was calling for him. Beethoven expired in 1827 and later died for this.

The Greeks were a highly sculptured people, and without them we wouldn't have history. The Greeks also had myths. A myth is a female moth.

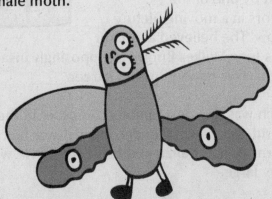

Astronomy

Five planets can be seen with the naked eye: Jupiter, Mars, Mercury, Saturn and Venus.

The Sea of Waves, the Sea of Cleverness, the Sea of Clouds and the Sea of Islands are all found on the moon.

Galileo went blind – probably because of his constant gazing at the sun through his telescope.

In the 1600s, French astronomer Adrien Auzout considered building a telescope that was 300 metres long. He thought the magnification would be so great he would see animals on the moon.

The moon weighs 81,000 trillion tons (approximately!).

Halley's comet last appeared in 1986 and won't appear again until 2061.

Two objects have struck the earth with

enough force to destroy a city. Each object, one in 1908 and one in 1947, struck regions of Siberia. Not one human being was hurt either time.

If it were possible to drive through space at 75 miles per hour, you could reach the sun in a little over 142 years. But at that same speed it would take more than 38 million years to reach the nearest star.

Are we there yet?

In 1989 the space shuttle *Discovery* carried 32 fertilized chicken eggs into orbit.

The surface speed record on the moon is 10.56 miles per hour. It was set in a lunar rover.

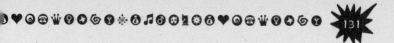

Dishes from around the world

Wasp Pupae (Japan)

Silkworm Omelette (China)

Sheep's Feet with Yoghurt (Turkey)

Stuffed Pig's Stomach (Hungary)

Grilled Snakemeat (Japan)

Polynesian Seaworm (Samoa)

Weasels (Japan)

Boiled Lamb's Head (North Africa)

Barbecued Cow Heart (Peru)

Baked Armadillo (served in the shell) (USA)

Fried Mole Cricket (Vietnam)

Monkeys' Heads (Japan)

Pig's Feet with Bananas (Philippines)

Lambs' Brains Tacos (Mexico)

Banana Worm Bread (Iowa State University, USA)

Stuffed Frogs (Philippines)

Earthworm Broth (China)

Giant Bullfrog and Pineapple Salad (USA)

Fried Cactus Caterpillars (Mexico)

Fried Grasshopper (China)

Locust Dumplings (North Africa)

Roasted Caterpillars (Laos)

Some of Homer Simpson's 'lifelong dreams'

Seeing a car shaped like a bowling pin.

Managing a beautiful country & western singer.

Living in the wilderness.

Becoming a monorail conductor.

Running out onto the baseball field during a game.

Becoming a blackjack dealer.

Being a contestant on *The Gong Show*.

Living under the sea.

Working in a bowling alley.

Working from home.

Owning the Dallas Cowboys.

Being the next Thomas Edison.

Becoming a hippy.

Ending crime and injustice.

Bowling a perfect game.

Getting rid of Bart.

Being a rock star.

Extraordinary frauds

THE BANK THAT NEVER WAS In 1908 Joseph 'Yellow Kid' Weil went into partnership with Fred Buckminster, a plain clothes policeman, who had once arrested him. Together, they rented an abandoned bank in Indiana and filled it with conmen who pretended to be wealthy investors – so fooling people into depositing their money in the bank.

PILTDOWN MAN In 1912, in a gravel pit near Piltdown Common in East Sussex, Charles

Dawson unearthed what was called 'the missing link' between man and ape. As time went by, its authenticity was doubted. In 1953 tests proved that the teeth of the skeleton had been filed down and stained to make it look older.

HITLER: THE RETURN In 1946 William H. Johnson, a miner from Kentucky, wrote to people all over the US pretending to be Adolf Hitler, telling them of his plan to take over the country and asking them to please send him some money. Incredibly, he managed to collect $15,000 before he was discovered.

SHAKESPEARE: THE RETURN In 1796 William Ireland managed to convince the scholars of England that he had 'discovered' two unknown Shakespeare plays – one of which was performed at Drury Lane. In fact, Ireland had written the plays himself. He admitted his con in 1797 but went unpunished.

THE GIANT MAN FOSSIL In 1868 William Newell and George Hull made a fortune by exhibiting what they said was the fossil of a giant man. They fooled many scientists. In fact, they had hired a stonemason to make the 'fossil' from gypsum and had stained it with sulphuric acid and ink to age it artificially.

SCRAP THE EIFFEL TOWER In 1925 the con artist Victor Lustig twice 'sold' the Eiffel Tower for scrap.

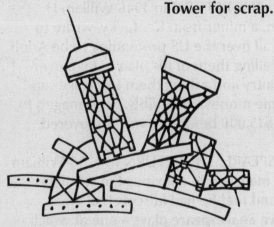

ANYONE WANT TO BUY A WHITE HOUSE? In 1925 Scotsman Arthur Ferguson persuaded several American tourists to pay £6,000 for Trafalgar Square and £1,000 for Big Ben. He then went to Washington, where he managed to sell a 99-year lease on the White House! Eventually, he was arrested and sent to prison for five years.

Weather

A one-day weather forecast requires about 10 billion mathematical calculations.

According to folklore, if a cat sleeps with all four paws tucked under its body, it means that cold weather is imminent.

In Bangladesh in 1988, 92 people were killed by giant hailstones weighing up to 1kg.

Lightning strikes the earth about 200 times a second.

Eurovision

The first contest was held in Lugano, Switzerland, on 24 May 1956. Seven countries participated – each submitting two songs (the only time this has happened). The host nation won.

In 1974 The Wombles provided entertainment during the interval. 20 years later, Riverdance was featured in the interval and became a worldwide phenomenon.

In 1978 Norway became the first country to receive 'nul points'. Four years later, Finland also hit zero with a song protesting about the building of a nuclear power station. In 2003 Jemini became the first UK act not to get a single point.

The country with the longest losing streak is Portugal. They first entered in 1964 and have not yet won.

When Katrina and the Waves won for Britain in 1997, they received the highest number of

top marks ever awarded to any song in the contest's history.

A staggering 95 per cent of the Danish viewing public tuned in to watch the 2001 contest.

ABBA are, of course, the most famous of all Eurovision acts, but before they won with 'Waterloo', they tried and failed to win the Swedish national selection competition with 'Ring Ring' in 1973.

Italy boycotted the 1981 contest, saying that it was too old-fashioned.

The 1991 contest was held in Italy. Unfortunately, no one thought to check that the two Italian presenters could speak English. They couldn't, and the show confused a lot of viewers.

The 1983 Turkish entry, 'Opera', consisted entirely of the word 'opera' being repeated over and over.

Around the world

All pilots on international flights identify themselves in English, regardless of their country of origin.

27 per cent of all journeys taken in the Netherlands are on a bicycle (this compares to just 2 per cent of journeys in the UK).

More Japanese and Chinese people die on the fourth of the month than on any other dates. The reason may be that they are 'scared to death' by the number four. The words for 'four' and 'death' sound alike in both Chinese and Japanese.

Volk's electric railway, which runs along Brighton's seafront, is the oldest operating electric railway in the world.

More than 1000 different languages are spoken in Africa.

On average in the West, people move house every seven years.

The global trade in counterfeit goods is worth about $340 billion a year.

Surtsey, just off the coast of Iceland, became the world's newest island when it was created by a volcanic eruption in 1963.

The Amazon rainforest produces half the world's oxygen supply.

Worldwide there are more statues of Joan of Arc than of anyone else. France alone has about 40,000.

The average French citizen eats 500 snails a year.

The original Guinness Brewery in Dublin, Ireland, has a 6000-year lease.

Australians are the heaviest gamblers in the world. An estimated 82 per cent of them bet regularly.

There's one gun for every ten people on earth.

Of all the world's land that is owned, just 1 per cent is owned by women.

Tristan da Cunha is the world's most remote settlement, being 2,334km away from its nearest neighbours.

The world's average school year is 200 days. In the US it is 180 days; in Sweden it is 170 days; in Japan it is 243 days.

Invented by women

Bulletproof vest, fire escape, windshield
wiper, laser printer, sewing machine,
alphabet block, underwater telescope, cotton
sewing thread (awarded the very first US
patent), cordless phone, pulsar (discovered
rather than invented), condensed milk, space
suit, TV dinner, Jell-O, Barbie, chocolate-
chip cookie, circular saw, dishwasher,
disposable nappy, electric hot-water heater,
ironing board, crash helmet, life raft, medical
syringe, rolling pin, rotary engine, Scotchgard
fabric protector

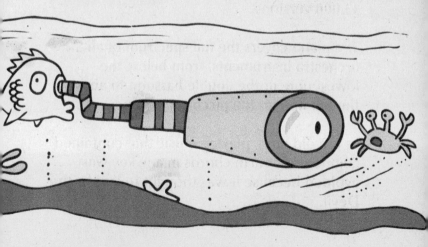

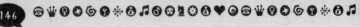

Music

The world's most extraordinary musical instrument was made in France in the 15th century. A long row of spikes was connected to a keyboard. Under each spike was a pig, arranged according to the pitch of its oink.

The Nutcracker was one of Tchaikovsky's most successful compositions but he didn't rate it at all.

'Summertime' by George Gershwin is the most recorded song of all time, with over 13,000 versions.

The piano covers the full spectrum of all orchestra instruments, from below the lowest note of the double bassoon to above the top note of the piccolo.

In the old days, playing music that contained augmented fourth chords in any key was avoided because it was thought to invoke the Devil.

Some 10 per cent of all the recorded music sold worldwide is bought and sold in Britain.

After Beethoven went deaf, he could still 'hear' his music by resting one end of a stick on the piano and holding the other end in his teeth and feeling the vibrations.

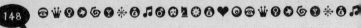

The human body

The sensitivity of the human eye is so keen that on a clear moonless night a person standing on a mountain can see a match being struck as far away as 50 miles (80km).

Humans, if they are very sensitive to taste, can detect sweetness in a solution of one part sugar to 200 parts water. Some moths and butterflies can detect sweetness when the ratio is one to 300,000.

The attachment of the human skin to muscles is what causes dimples.

There are 60,000 miles (96,540km) of blood vessels in the human body. If they were laid end to end, they would encircle the earth two and a half times.

The tips of the fingers and the soles of the feet are covered by a thick, tough layer of skin called the stratum corneum.

The brain is not sensitive to pain. Headache

pain originates in the nerves, muscles and tissues surrounding the skull, not the brain. If a brain is cut into, the person feels no pain.

Humans have three colour receptors in their eyes, while goldfish have four, and mantis shrimp have ten.

There are 45 miles of nerves in the skin of a human being.

The human brain continues sending out electrical wave signals for up to 37 hours after death.

Most people have legs of slightly different lengths.

The body's largest internal organ is the small intestine, at an average length of 6 metres.

The large intestine is only a sixth of the size of the small intestine.

The hydrochloric acid in the human stomach is strong enough to dissolve a nail.

It takes only 15 watts of electricity going through a human body to stop the heart. Common light bulbs run on about 25 to 75 watts of electricity.

The knee is the most easily injured of all the joints in the body.

Our skin is only about as deep as the tip of a ballpoint pen.

Humans share a third of their DNA with lettuce.

Non-drivers

David Mitchell
Sir David Attenborough
Claudia Schiffer
Gordon Brown
Gareth Gates
Ricky Gervais
Kate Beckinsale

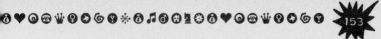

Amphibians

All known amphibians and reptiles that live below the surface of the earth are carnivores, eating creatures such as worms and ants.

The Asian giant salamander is the largest amphibian. It lives in the cold streams of China and Japan and can reach lengths of 1.5 metres and weights of 40kg.

The eggs of the marsupial frog are laid in a pouch on the mother's back and the young hatch out in a zip-like fashion from the pouch.

20 tons of toads are killed on Britain's roads every year.

The poison arrow frog has enough poison to kill 2,200 people. Poison arrow frogs lose their poison when they're kept in captivity because the source of the poison is a chemical found in small beetles that only exist in the wild.

Several salamanders make squeaking noises when disturbed. The Pacific giant sends out a scream and a rattle to ward off enemies.

Some salamander species arch their back and raise their head to imitate a poisonous snake and deter an attacker that way.

The sitatunga antelope is amphibious (but not an amphibian). Its hooves are adapted for water and are awkward on dry land.

Celebrity trivia

Britney Spears has had a hotel suite named after her (at the Onyx Hotel, Boston).

When Pete Doherty was 17, he won a competition and was chosen to travel with the British Council to Russia to perform his poetry.

Paris Hilton trademarked the phrase 'That's hot!'

Brad Pitt studied Journalism at university.

Leonardo DiCaprio was once guest editor of *National Geographic Kids* magazine.

Alexander Graham Bell, inventor of the telephone, never phoned his wife or mother as both were deaf.

Whoopi Goldberg's first grandchild was born on her 35th birthday. Whoopi Goldberg got her first name because she had a problem with flatulence.

James McAvoy is a fire-eater.

Ricky Gervais's chosen items for *Room 101*, a programme in which a celebrity is invited to send the things he or she hates most into oblivion, were Children in Restaurants, Lateness, Children in Need, Caravan Holidays and Noisy People. (Caravan Holidays was the only one that didn't go through.)

In 2006 Cristiano Ronaldo opened a fashion store, CR7, in his home town of Funchal (on the island of Madeira). His elder sisters manage the store.

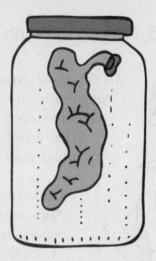

Lindsay Lohan keeps her appendix in a jar in her room.

Elvis Presley never gave an encore.

Albert Einstein, Lewis Carroll and Charles Darwin all married their cousins.

Vince Vaughn's sisters also have the initials V.V.

Cameron Diaz, Halle Berry, Demi Moore and Justin Timberlake are all keen ten-pin bowlers.

Cartoons and animation

In 1938 Joe Shuster and Jerry Siegel sold all rights to the comic-strip character Superman to their publishers for $130.

Clark Kent, Superman's alter ego, was derived from the names of the Hollywood stars Clark Gable and Kent Taylor.

Walt Disney named Mickey Mouse after the child star Mickey Rooney, whose mother he dated.

Mickey Mouse's birthday is November 18th.

Mickey Mouse is known as Topolino in Italy.

Scooby Doo's real first name is Scoobert.

Dr William Moulton Marston, the man who created the comic-book character Wonder Woman, also invented the lie-detector test.

The most common set of initials for Superman's friends and enemies is L.L.

Bart Simpson's hair has nine spikes.

Homer Simpson's pin number is 7431.

The comic strip 'Peanuts' is known in Denmark as 'Radishes'.

Captain Euro was a superhero commissioned by the European Union to promote itself. His arch-enemy is Dr D. Vider.

Christmas

The average Briton devotes 15 hours a year to Christmas shopping. Around 25 per cent of that time is spent in queues.

The Christmas song 'Jingle Bells' was originally composed in 1857 as a Thanksgiving song.

The Queen and the Duke of Edinburgh send some 850 Christmas cards a year.

The reason why robins are associated with Christmas is because postmen, who wore red, were known as robins, and so many Christmas cards depicted robins delivering cards.

It's St Francis of Assisi we have to thank for introducing Christmas carols to church services.

It wasn't until 440 that 25th December was first celebrated as the birthday of Christ.

Santa Claus is called Babbo Natale in Italy.

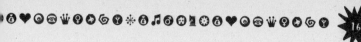

More than eight million Christmas trees were sold in Britain last year.

Holly is associated with Christmas because the sharply pointed leaves symbolized the thorns in Christ's crown and the red berries symbolized his blood.

There are 178 legs in the song 'The Twelve Days of Christmas': 1 partridge, 2 doves, 3 hens, 4 colly birds, 6 geese, 7 swans, 8 maids with a cow each, 9 ladies, 10 lords, 11 pipers and 12 drummers.

The Christmas holidays are the busiest time for American plastic surgeons.

The Christmas Day 1986 edition of *EastEnders* attracted a record audience of 30.15 million people.

Around 16 million turkeys were sold in the UK last Christmas.

Lipstick names

Amour, Firecracker, Censored, Strawberry Fair, Corsaire, Nutmeg, Moon Beam, Neon Nude, Cool Candy, Passionate Pink, Mad Mauve, Risky Ruby, Portobello Plum, True Terracotta, Hot Honey, Barely Blush, Crazy Caramel, Too Truffle, Rolling Stone, Warm Platinum, Golden Spice, Chocoholic, Whisper, Fig, Parma Argent, Buttermilk, Sherbet Twist, Wine & Dine, Just Peachy, Hearts a Fire, So Cinnamon, In the Nude, Summer Daze, Let's Go Crazy

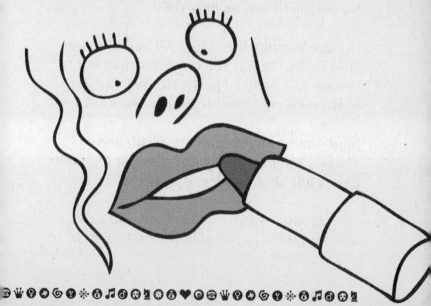

US presidents

No (former) American president has ever died in the month of May.

Prior to the Second World War, when guards were posted at the fence, anyone could wander right up to the front door of the White House – the president's home.

Every president who has had a beard has been Republican.

No president was an only child.

George Washington (1789–97) had wooden false teeth. He was the only president not to belong to a political party. He was also the only president to be elected unanimously.

John Adams (the second president) and Thomas Jefferson (the third) died on the same day: 4 July (Independence Day) 1826.

John Quincy Adams (1825–9) owned a pet alligator, which he kept in the east room of

the White House. His wife, Louisa Adams, was the first (and only) foreign-born First Lady of the US; she was born in London.

In 1845 President Andrew Jackson's pet parrot was removed from his funeral for swearing.

In 1849 David Atchison became president of the United States for just one day.

Ulysses S. Grant (1869–77) was tone-deaf and once said: 'I only know two tunes. One of them is "Yankee Doodle" and the other isn't.'

James Garfield (1881) could write in Greek with one hand while writing in Latin with the other. Garfield, who lived in the White House with his mother, often gave campaign speeches in German.

At up to 150kg, William Taft (1909–13) was the heaviest president and once had the misfortune to get stuck in the White House bathtub. At just over 44kg, James Madison (1809–17) was the lightest president.

When Calvin Coolidge (1923–9) was being driven in a car, he would always insist the driver didn't exceed 16 mph. Coolidge's pets included a goose, a wallaby, a donkey, a lion cub, two cats and twelve dogs. He was sworn into office by his own father.

Herbert Hoover (1929–33) and his wife both spoke fluent Chinese. Herbert Hoover is the only US president to turn over his entire annual salary to charity.

Lyndon Johnson's (1963–8) family all had the initials LBJ: Lyndon Baines Johnson, Lady Bird Johnson, Linda Bird Johnson and Lucy Baines

Johnson. His dog was called Little Beagle Johnson. President Johnson died just one mile from the house in which he was born.

Grover Cleveland (1893–7) answered the White House phone himself. He also worked briefly as an executioner before becoming president, and hanged at least two convicted criminals.

There are lots of photographs of Abraham Lincoln (1861–5), but not one of him smiling.

Barack Obama, the current president, is the only president there has ever been whose surname starts and ends with a vowel.

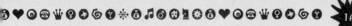

Written by pupils in science tests

When you breathe, you inspire. When you do not breathe, you expire.

H_2O is hot water, and CO_2 is cold water.

Blood flows down one leg and up the other.

A fossil is an extinct animal. The older it is, the more extinct it is.

The moon is a planet just like the earth, only it is even deader.

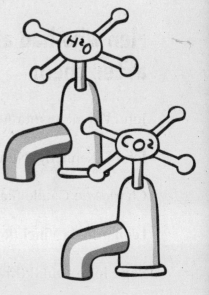

Mushrooms always grow in damp places and so they look like umbrellas.

The tides are a fight between the earth and moon. All water tends towards the moon, because there is no water in the moon, and nature abhors a vacuum. I forget where the sun joins in this fight.

To remove dust from the eye, pull the eye down over the nose.

To keep milk from turning sour, keep it in the cow.

Men who had airports named after them

John Wayne (Santa Ana)

John F. Kennedy (New York)

Charles de Gaulle (Paris)

Leonardo da Vinci (Rome)

Pope John Paul II (Krakow)

Marco Polo (Venice)

Jomo Kenyatta (Nairobi)
Pablo Picasso (Malaga)

John Lennon (Liverpool)

George Bush (Houston)

Louis Armstrong (New Orleans)

Wolfgang Amadeus Mozart (Salzburg)

George Best (Belfast)

The names of things you didn't know had names

Adelaster: meaning 'unknown star' in Greek, this is the name given to newly discovered plants awaiting classification by botanists.

Brannock device: the metal instrument used in shoe shops to measure feet.

Brassard: a band worn around the arm.

Buccula: a person's double chin.

Drupelets: the bumps on raspberries.

Epizootic: an animal epidemic.

Harp: the metal part of a lamp that surrounds the bulb and supports the shade.

Octothorpe: the # symbol on a computer keyboard.

Tang: the part of the blade that extends into

the handle of a knife.

Tines: the prongs on forks.

Toque: a chef's tall hat.

Vamp: the upper front top of a shoe.

Walla: a sound engineer's term for the murmur of a crowd in the background.

12 English icons

In 2006 the Department for Culture launched
a project – *Icons: A Portrait of England*.
Art experts and academics suggested the
following 12 icons to represent England:

Alice in Wonderland
The Angel of the North
A cup of tea
SS *Empire Windrush*
The FA Cup
Henry VIII by Holbein
The King James Bible
Punch and Judy
The Routemaster bus
Stonehenge
The Spitfire
Blake's 'Jerusalem'

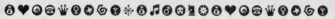

The world

Every day is a holiday somewhere in the world.

The earth gets 100 tons heavier every day due to falling space dust.

Lake Manitou on Manitoulin Island in the middle of Lake Huron in Canada is the largest lake on an island within a lake in the world.

There is enough salt in the oceans to cover all the continents with a layer 150 metres thick.

There is enough stone in the Great Wall of China to build a 2.43-metre-high wall encircling the globe at the equator.

The earth's crust has an average depth of 24km.

The lifetime of the sun's light is estimated at 109 years (i.e. 10,000,000,000).

Every year the sun loses 360 million tons.

All the land mass of the earth – and more – could fit into the Pacific Ocean.

It takes 8.5 minutes for light to get from the sun to earth.

China has more borders with other countries than any other country.

Over one million earths would fit in the sun.

There are more than 1,200 million trillion

litres of water on earth.

The Sutter Buttes in California is the smallest mountain range in the world.

At just over 36 metres, the D river in Lincoln City, Oregon, is the shortest river in the world. It would seem it also has the shortest name.

There have been fewer people to go below 2km in the sea than have been on the moon.

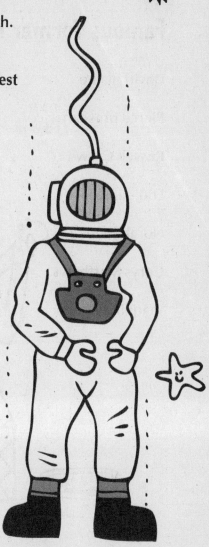

Famous former buskers

David Blaine

Pierce Brosnan

Russell Crowe

Eddie Izzard

Norah Jones

Cerys Matthews

Joaquin Phoenix

Celebrities who have owned pet rats

Angelina Jolie

Nicole Richie

Jamie Lee Curtis

Rupert Grint

Kim Basinger

Clint Eastwood

John Cleese

Pink

Luxuries chosen on *Desert Island Discs*

Desert Island Discs is a long-running radio show in which celebrity 'castaways' are invited to choose eight records, a book and a luxury item to take with them.

Notting Hill Pizza Express – Richard Curtis

Strong sunblock – Nicole Kidman

Mirror – Simon Cowell

Pair of swimming goggles with prescription lenses – Chris Evans

His guitar – Colin Firth

A pack of cards – Bill Bailey

Large supply of chocolate – Dame Kelly Holmes

Large pot of French mustard – Boris Johnson
His favourite London restaurant – Matt Lucas

**Vat of Novocaine (a pain-killer) – Ricky
Gervais**

Shaving kit – Matthew Pinsent

Anchored yacht – George Clooney

Cappuccino maker – John Malkovich

Fresh vanilla pod – Gordon Ramsay

Potato seeds – Vic Reeves

Piano – Meera Syal

Piano – Paul Whitehouse

Two tape recorders – Rolf Harris

A car to clean – Rowan Atkinson

Electrical device to heat shaving foam – Billy Connolly

The laws of the land (so he could break them) – Benjamin Zephaniah

Grand piano – Jools Holland

Motorway service station – Noel Edmonds

Classical guitar – Tony Blair

Unlimited paper and a pen – J. K. Rowling

Odds against . . .

. . . being killed by a bee sting: one in 6 million.

. . . hitting two holes-in-one during the same round of golf: one in 8 million.

. . . every match in a full Premier League programme finishing in a 0–0 draw: one in 60 million.

. . . being on a plane hijacked by terrorists twice in the same year: one in 150 million.

The 10 distinct kinds of laughter

Amused laugh

Joy laugh

Sympathetic laugh

Polite laugh

Relief laugh

Disappointment laugh

Embarrassed laugh

Stressed laugh

Comment laugh

Ironical laugh

Tomatoes

Tomatoes originate in the Andes in South America.

They were first cultivated by the Aztecs and Incas as early as AD 700.

Tomatoes arrived in Europe in the 16th century – probably brought back from Central America by Spanish Conquistadors.

The first cultivated tomatoes were cherry-sized and yellow and were called golden apples. That's why the Italian for tomato is pomodoro.

The French were convinced that tomatoes had aphrodisiac properties and called them pommes d'amour (love apples).

Tomato juice takes away the smell of a skunk.

It wasn't until the 19th century – and the large-scale production of sheet glass – that commercial tomato cultivation began in Britain. The first glasshouses were built in Essex and Kent.

Tomatoes are cultivated as far north as Iceland and as far south as the Falkland Islands. Tomato seedlings have even been grown in space.

The human condition

You can't bend your little finger without moving the finger next to it. (Just try!)

The average baby uses a total of 5,800 nappies.

A healthy adult can draw in about 3.3 to 4.9 litres of air at a single breath, but at rest only about 5 per cent of this volume is used.

Certain sounds in the English language are real germ spreaders, particularly the sounds of F, P, T, D and S.

A baby knows its mother's voice and is able to distinguish it from others while still in the womb.

According to a handwriting analyst, people who write with large letters have a lot of ambition.

Humans can't taste water – although some animals can. We taste the chemicals and impurities in the water but not the water itself.

Happy events – like family celebrations or evenings with friends – boost the immune system for the following two days.

Proportional to our weight, humans are stronger than horses.

You can't sneeze in your sleep.

One human hair can support 3kg.

A newborn baby sees the world upside down. It takes some time for the baby's brain to learn to turn the picture the right way up.

According to research, women are enticed to buy more if they hear the sound of heels clicking on the floor.

Vegetarian women are more likely to give birth to baby girls than to baby boys.

85 per cent of people can curl their tongue into a 'U' shape.

Less than 1 per cent of a fart is made up of stinky stuff but that's smelly enough to make it unpleasant.

People whose initials spell out GOD or ACE are likely to live longer than people whose initials spell out words like APE, PIG or RAT.

The average fart releases about 100ml of gas.

Words of Yiddish or Jewish origin

Bagel: a ring-shaped bread roll (ideal with 'lox' – see below)

Chutzpah: cheek, audacity, effrontery

Glitch: a minor malfunction

Klutz: clumsy person

Kvetch: complain, gripe

Lox: smoked salmon

Mensch: decent human being

Nosh: snack

Schlep: to drag or carry (something); make a tedious journey

Schmaltz: excessive sentimentality

Schmendrik: fool

Schmooze: chat, butter up

Schmutter: (cheap) clothing

Shtick: comic theme; defining habit

Spiel: sales pitch

Clubs that supplied players to the England team

There was a time (in the 19th century) before Chelsea, Manchester United, Liverpool and Arsenal dominated the game . . .

Uxbridge
1st Surrey Rifles
Barnes
Hertfordshire Rangers
Harrow Chequers
Swifts
Owlerton
Sheffield Heeley
Upton Park
Pilgrims

Bingo calls

1	Kelly's eye
2	One little duck
5	Man alive
9	Doctor's orders
11	Legs eleven
16	Never been kissed
22	Two little ducks
25	Duck and dive
26	Bed and breakfast
27	Little duck with a crutch
30	Burlington Bertie
39	Those famous steps

44   **Droopy drawers**

55   **Snakes alive**

59   **Brighton line**

66   Clickety click

88   **Two fat ladies**

90   Top of the shop

Things from abroad

Danish pastry, **German measles**, Brazil nuts,
Mexican stand-off, Dutch elm disease,
Chinese whispers, Russian salad, **Indian gift**,
French leave, **Russian roulette**, Swiss roll,
Hong Kong flu, **Cuban heels**, Mexican wave,
Greek urn, Singapore sling, **Dutch uncle**,
Turkish delight, **Indian tonic water**, French
bread, **Maltese cross**, Italian vermouth,
Panama hat, Spanish omelette

Marine life

Seals hold their breath while they sleep on the surface of the water.

Female whales live twice as long as male whales.

Handicapped dolphins can survive independently. A blind, deaf and mute nine year old bottlenose was found in Californian waters. It was monitored for seven years and managed perfectly well without normal communication.

Bottlenose dolphins can mimic the sounds other dolphins make underwater.

Dolphins jump out of the water to conserve energy as it's easier to move through the air than through the water.

Humpback whales use language involving syntax and grammar in the songs they sing.

Sea otters inhabit water but never get wet because they have two coats of fur.

Sharks can be dangerous even before they are born. Scientist Stewart Springer was bitten by a sand tiger shark embryo while he was examining its pregnant mother.

Walruses have astonishing sucking power and can suck the brains of seal pups out through their nostrils.

About ten times more men than women are attacked by sharks.

The embryos of tiger sharks fight each other while in their mother's womb, the survivor being the baby shark that is born.

The cookie-cutter shark is so aggressive it even attacks nuclear submarines.

Walruses use their long downward tusks to help them get about. Their zoological name means 'toothwalk'.

There were once more sea lions on earth than people.

Things that are brand names

Tannoy, Li-Lo, Jiffy Bag, Optic, Plasticine, Biro, Crimplene, Hoover, Fibreglass, Babygro, Sellotape, Cellophane, Portakabin, Catseyes, Rawlplug, Jacuzzi, Spam, Perspex, Calor Gas, Formica, Yo-Yo, Tarmac

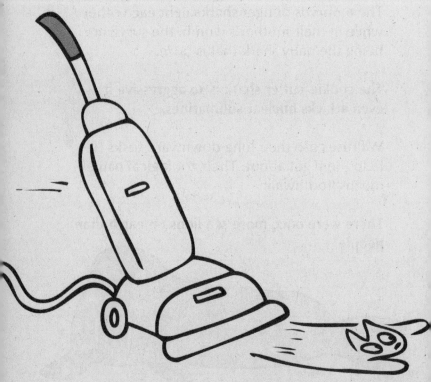

Toilets

By the end of this year, approximately 22
billion rolls of toilet paper will have been
used around the world.

The French use less toilet paper than any
other Europeans; the Swedes use the most,
while the British are sixth in the loo-roll table.
In total, we Britons use nearly 1.5 billion loo
rolls, more than 200,000 tons a year.

American civil servants' pay cheques are
recycled to make toilet rolls.

American researchers spent $100,000 on
making the discovery that three out of four
people hang their toilet rolls so that the paper
is pulled down to be torn off rather than up.

The world's oldest piece of toilet paper
– thought to be 1,200 years old – was found
buried under an Israeli garage.

An American toilet manufacturer in California
has created loo rolls made from hay. It is not

known whether this is the same Californian company that in 1992 started selling 'camouflage' toilet paper for hunters to use so that fellow hunters don't mistake them for whitetailed deer.

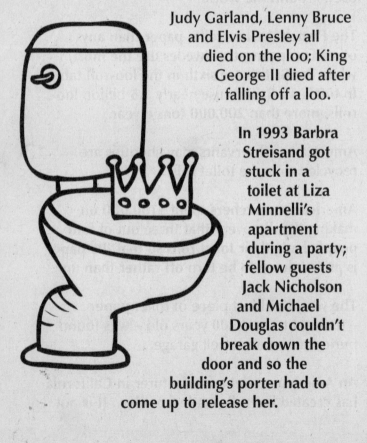

Judy Garland, Lenny Bruce and Elvis Presley all died on the loo; King George II died after falling off a loo.

In 1993 Barbra Streisand got stuck in a toilet at Liza Minnelli's apartment during a party; fellow guests Jack Nicholson and Michael Douglas couldn't break down the door and so the building's porter had to come up to release her.

Jack Nicholson has a dead rattlesnake embedded in the clear plastic seat of his toilet.

Sir Winston Churchill did not believe in using toilet seats. He had them for his guests, but when his plumber asked him what sort of seat he would have on his own loo, he responded, 'I have no need of such things.'

Onlys

The Iolani Palace of Oahu in Hawaii is the only royal palace in the United States.

The only purple animal is the South African blesbok.

Cuttlefish are the only creatures that have W-shaped pupils. This allows them to see backwards and forwards at the same time.

The USA is the only non-metric country in the world.

King Kong is the only movie to have its sequel

– *Son of Kong* – released the same year (1933).

The only time the human population declined was in the years following 1347, the start of the epidemic of the plague 'Black Death' in Europe.

The only fruit that has its seeds on the outside is the strawberry.

Former Prime Minister William E. Gladstone and Dr Barnado were the only people ever to have their coffins transported on the London Underground.

The chihuahua is the only breed of dog that is born with an incomplete skull (it has a little hole that closes as the dog matures).

Sir Isaac Newton's only recorded utterance while he was a member of parliament was a request to open the window.

The Parisian McDonald's has the only white 'golden arches' in the world (it was thought that yellow was too tacky).

The McDonald's at Toronto's 'SkyDome' is the only McDonald's location that sells hot dogs.

The common goldfish is the only creature that can see both infra-red and ultra-violet light.

Pope Adrian IV (Nicholas Breakspeare) was the only English Pope (1154–9).

The sea otter is the only non-primate that can use tools to break open hard shells to access food.

The only bone in the human body not connected to another is the hyoid, a V-shaped bone located at the base of the tongue between the mandible (jaw) and the voice box. Its function is to support the tongue and its muscles.

The donkey is the only domestic animal to have originated in Africa.

Lichfield is the only British city with all its letters in the first half of the alphabet.

There are only three world capitals that begin with the letter O in English: Ottawa, Canada; Oslo, Norway; and Ouagadougou, Burkina Faso.

A cow's only sweat glands are in its nose.

Pure Trivia

Before the 16th century, shoes didn't have heels. Queen Elizabeth I had them added to give the royal family additional stature.

It would take about 3,085,209,600,000 rolls of wallpaper to cover the Sahara desert.

Eel-skin wallets have been known to demagnetize credit cards.

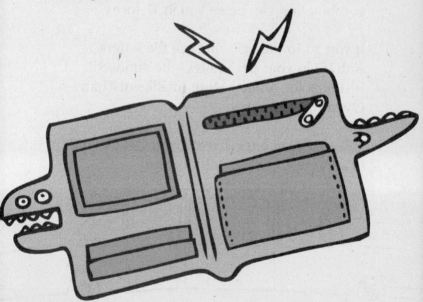

Sir Walter Scott named his dog Hamlet.

Most dinosaurs lived to be more than 100 years old.

Bigamy is when someone gets married while they're already married to someone else. A man named Giovanni Vigliotto married 104 women in 14 different countries between 1949 and 1981.

If done perfectly, any Rubik's cube combination can be solved in 17 turns.

If you go to the vet's and see the letters AMITO in your pet's notes – be annoyed! It stands for Animal More Intelligent Than Owner.

Salvador Dali once arrived at an art exhibition in a limousine filled with turnips.

When fashionable Parisian women of the late 18th century went out in blustery weather, they wore a lightning rod attached to their hats.

In the 13th century it was customary to baptize children with beer.

The average life span of an umbrella is under two years.

The parachute was invented before the aeroplane.

There are 294 steps in the Leaning Tower of Pisa.

In 1994 an Austrian woman was killed when her underwired bra was struck by lightning.

Roy Cleveland Sullivan, a US National Park ranger in Shenandoah National Park in Virginia, survived no fewer than seven lightning strikes between 1942 and 1977. The odds against this happening have been calculated at 16-septillion to one (16 followed by 24 zeros).

All known mammals have tongues.

Statistically, couples are more likely to break up on 12 January than on any other day of the year.

Ghosts appear in four Shakespeare plays: Julius Caesar, Richard III, Hamlet and Macbeth.

If you took 500g of cobwebs and spread them out in a straight line, the thread would go round the earth twice.

Henry Ford produced the Model T Ford in black only because the black paint available at the time was the fastest to dry.

Counting at one digit per second, it would take more than 11½ days and nights of non-stop counting to reach one million.

An 11-year-old American boy farted 217 times in five minutes on a radio call-in show.

Plants

Four times as many plants live on the land as in the sea.

Of the world's 15,000 known species of orchid, 20 per cent can be found in Brazil.

The titan arum flower is the largest flower in the world but gives off a horrible odour of rotting flesh when it blooms.

In the summer, walnuts get a tan.

Young children are poisoned by houseplants more often than by detergents and other chemicals.

The welwitschia plant is considered a living fossil and can live for up to 1,000 years.

About 7,000 cherries grow on the average cherry tree.

The ancient Greeks believed ivy to be the sign of everlasting love.

Paper can be made from asparagus.

Up to 3,000 species of tree have been catalogued in a single square mile of the Amazon jungle.

The world's oldest rose is located outside Hildeshiem cathedral in Germany and is thought to be over 1,000 years old.

Macadamia nuts are toxic to dogs.

The largest living organism ever found is a honey mushroom that covers 3.4 square miles of land in the Blue Mountains of eastern Oregon – and it's still growing.

Wonderfully named characters from the world of Jeeves and Bertie Wooster, created by P. G. Wodehouse

Barmy Fotheringay-Phipps,
Stilton Cheesewright,
Pongo Twistleton-
Twistleton, Gussie
Fink-Nottle, Biscuit
Biskerton, Stiffy
Stiffham, Catsmeat
Potter-Pirbright,
Dogface Rainsby,
Oofy Prosser,
Freddie Fitch-Fitch

Army ranks and how they correspond in the navy and air force

ARMY	NAVY	RAF
Field Marshal	Admiral of the Fleet	Marshal of the RAF
General	Admiral	Air Chief Marshal
Lieutenant-General	Vice Admiral	Air Marshal
Major-General	Rear Admiral	Air Vice-Marshal
Brigadier	Commodore	Air Commodore
Colonel	Captain	Group Captain
Lieutenant-Colonel	Commander	Wing Commander
Major	Lieutenant-Commander	Squadron Leader
Captain	Lieutenant	Flight Lieutenant
Lieutenant	Sub-Lieutenant	Flying Officer

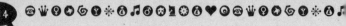

Animals that became verbs

Fox – to trick someone.

Pig – to devour food hurriedly and without manners.

Dog – to follow someone, particularly their footsteps.

Wolf – to eat ravenously.

Badger – to pester someone.

Monkey – to play around with someone or something.

Snake – to crawl on your belly.

Hog – to take all of something or keep it for yourself.

Rabbit – to talk incessantly.

Stag – to sell a new issue of shares immediately.

Ape – to impersonate someone or something.

Animal adjectives

You probably know that a cat (and all things to do with a cat) is described as 'feline' and a dog as 'canine'. Here's how other creatures can be described.

Ape – simian
Bear – ursine
Bird – avian
Bull – taurine
Cow – bovine
Elephant – elephantine
Fish – piscine
Horse – equine
Lion – leonine
Oyster – ostracine
Pig – porcine
Rabbit – lapine
Seahorse – hippocampine
Sheep – ovine
Wolf – lupine

Annual American events

St Stupid's Day Parade (celebrating the patron saint of the First Church of the Last Laugh)

Xtreme Rat Challenge

Frozen Dead Guy Days

Spamarama

The Great Mushroom Hunt Championships

Chitlin' Strut (festival based around chitterlings – boiled and fried pig intestines)

Big Mountain Furniture Race

International Whistlers Convention

Billy the Kid Tombstone Race

Hot Dog Eating Tournament

Former cheerleaders

Madonna

Sandra Bullock

Renée Zellweger (star cheerleader)

Cameron Diaz

Alicia Silverstone

Reese Witherspoon

Paris Hilton

Kirsten Dunst

Miley Cyrus

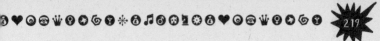
Britain's favourite paintings

As voted for in a 2005 BBC Radio 4 poll

The Fighting Temeraire Tugged To Her Last Berth To Be Broken Up by J.M.W. Turner

The Hay Wain by John Constable

A Bar at the Folies-Bergère by Edouard Manet

Sunflowers by Vincent Van Gogh

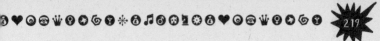

Mr and Mrs Clark and Percy by David Hockney

The Arnolfini Portrait by Jan Van Eyck

The Last of England by Ford Madox Brown

The Baptism of Christ by Piero della Francesca

A Rake's Progress III: The Orgy by William Hogarth

The Reverend Robert Walker Skating on Duddingston Loch by Sir Henry Raeburn

Animals

Galapagos tortoises were named after a type of Spanish saddle because of the shape of their shells.

Reindeer hair is hollow.

Tarsiers are little primates whose brains are smaller than their eyeballs.

There are about 1.5 million hedgehogs in the UK.

When a hippopotamus dies, other hippos surround the corpse and lick it – only leaving the corpse when pressure from hungry crocodiles gets too great.

The long-nosed bandicoot has its pouch on its back.

The orangutan eats very slowly. It can take 20 minutes to chew a single piece of fruit.

Beavers mate for life.

Wolves are capable of covering over 100 miles in a single day.

The star-nosed mole is the fastest-eating mammal in the world. Using its fleshy tentacles, it can eat a meal of worms in 227 milliseconds.

Sheep can recognize other sheep's faces and remember up to 50 individuals.

The cells that make up the antlers of a moose are the fastest-growing animal cells in nature.

Horses (and dogs) put two-thirds of their weight on their front legs when standing.

Animals evolved legs to walk underwater, not on land. Some types of fish appear to use their fins to walk along the seabed.

Ferrets have just one type of blood group – unlike most other mammals, which have several different types.

Giraffes never kneel.

Hedgehogs can climb trees (their spines protect them from injury if they fall).

The pronghorn antelope can run at up to 61 mph.

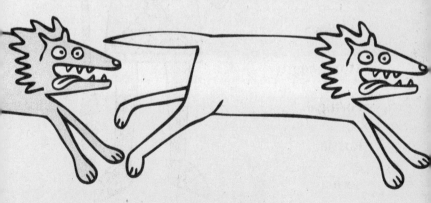

St George is the patron saint of . . .

England. He's also the patron saint of:

Canada

Ethiopia

Germany

Greece

Lithuania

Malta

Moldova

Montenegro

Portugal

Russia

Serbia

Sardines

The word 'SARDINE' refers to any of several species of small food fish of temperate waters that are also known as pilchards – especially when adult. Sardines are shoaling fish that live near the surface and feed on plankton. This ends the encyclopaedia definition.

Sardines are sensitive fish. They move away from their shoaling grounds and don't return for decades after naval battles.

Sardines as part of your diet can improve your memory – according to a study of children in 1987.

Sardines were sold for years in cans with keys that would inevitably break as you tried to turn them, leaving razor-sharp edges. This led to cut fingers, a lot of swearing, oil going everywhere and no sardines for tea. In the past few years they have been sold flat in cans with a ring-pull (like a soft drink) or standing up in a can which is opened with a tin opener (like a can of baked beans). In the dark days of the old-style sardine-can key, nearly half of the shoppers surveyed complained about sardine-can keys breaking off or cutting them.

The Norwegian city of Stavanger uses as its symbol and crest the key to a tin of sardines.

Traditionally sardines were encouraged to rise to the surface of the sea by the fishermen drumming their feet on the bottom of the boat. The foaming shoals would then be scooped up in large quantities.

In Britain, tinned sardines are one of our cheapest foodstuffs. If we want to describe someone as broke, we talk about them living on a diet of sardines.

The French take sardines seriously. They sell prime quality tinned sardines – skinned and boned, in extra virgin olive oil – and even vintage sardines: date-stamped with the year they were captured because good sardines improve in the can so long as the can is turned regularly. The French value sardines so highly they have a museum dedicated to them, in Sète, which features stuffed sardines, pictures of sardines and live sardines in tanks. The museum's creator said, 'The fish are part of our culture.'

Some 14 million tins of sardines – the equivalent of 5,400 tons – are sold annually in Britain.

Like all oily fish, sardines (especially fresh ones) are good for lowering cholesterol and are therefore an important guard against heart disease.

In Ipswich, Queensland, in Australia, sardines rained down from the sky in 1989. The fish were sucked up from the sea by a strong updraught of air and fell to the ground like hail. The local cats were said to be delighted.

In Marseille, France, a 4,500-piece jigsaw depicting a two-acre sardine was laid out by 30 people in one week in 1992.

In 1994 in Lima, Peru, 1,500 young people made a three-mile-long sardine sandwich in an attempt to get into the Peruvian *Guinness Book of Records*.

In 1995 millions of dead sardines were washed ashore along the Australian New South Wales coast, when a mystery illness led to them suffocating after mucus blocked their gills.

There's the true story of the young boy who was told by his teacher to write about the harmful effects of oil on fish for his homework. He wrote, 'My mummy opened a tin of sardines. The sardines were covered in oil and they were all dead.'

The European Patents Office says that the most commonly requested item among its 31 million patent documents is sardine-flavoured ice cream. A spokesman says, 'No one believes that it actually exists until they've called it up and seen it themselves.'

Some 'Fathers'

Herodotus – the Father of History
Sir Isaac Newton – the Father of Physics
Eratosthenes – the Father of Geography
Geoffrey Chaucer – the Father of English
   Literature
Charles Babbage – the Father of Computing
Hippocrates – the Father of Medicine
Pythagoras – the Father of Numbers

Food and drink

The average ear of corn has 800 kernels
arranged in 16 rows.

Chillies have been eaten in South America
since at least 7000 BC, and at one point were
used as currency.

Almonds are the oldest nuts in the world.

In ancient China, mouse meat was
considered a delicacy.

In ancient Egypt, the apricot was called the egg of the sun.

About a quarter of the food we buy gets thrown away.

The mango is the best-selling fruit in the world – and India is the world's biggest producer.

The world's biggest ever teabag was 4 by 3 metres, and made 11,000 cups of Earl Grey. It was made in 2003 to celebrate the company Twining's 300th birthday.

When consumed with a meal, orange juice helps the body absorb iron.

Bananas grow pointing upwards.

First Lady Eleanor Roosevelt (1933–45) ate three chocolate-covered garlic balls every morning. Her doctor suggested this would improve her memory.

An onion, an apple and a potato all have the same taste. The differences in flavour are caused by their smell.

You can make yoghurt from camel's milk but you can't make butter.

The left drumstick of a chicken is softer than the right drumstick.

Chocolate is the number-one ice-cream flavour in the world, beating vanilla and banana by three to one.

Olive oil is only made from green (as opposed to black) olives.

Unintentionally funny newspaper headlines

DAD WANTS BABY LEFT IN AEROPLANE

FLAMING TOILET SEAT CAUSES EVACUATION AT HIGH SCHOOL

PANDA MATING FAILS – VETERINARIAN TAKES OVER

TRAFFIC DEAD RISE SLOWLY

DRUNK GETS NINE MONTHS IN VIOLIN CASE

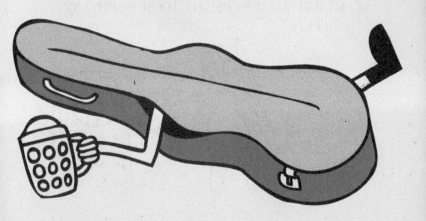

KICKING BABY CONSIDERED TO BE HEALTHY

TUNA BITING OFF WASHINGTON COAST

BLIND WOMAN GETS NEW KIDNEY FROM DAD SHE HASN'T SEEN IN YEARS

MAN WITH ONE ARM AND LEG CHEATS ON OTHER HALF

MILK DRINKERS ARE TURNING TO POWDER

DRUGS FINE FOR BUSINESSMAN

BABIES USED TO SNEAK DRUGS INTO PRISON

CEMETERY ALLOWS PEOPLE TO BE BURIED BY THEIR PETS

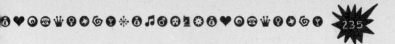

Around the world

The world's largest car park is in West Edmonton Mall in Edmonton, Canada. It has space for over 20,000 vehicles.

In Ivrea, Italy, people celebrate the beginning of Lent by throwing oranges at one another.

The population of Colombia doubles every 22 years.

Peru has more pyramids than Egypt.

Beijing has the world's largest Kentucky Fried Chicken restaurant.

Alaska has twice as many caribou as people.

57 per cent of journeys in the Dutch city of Groningen are made by bicycle.

Parmesan is the most shoplifted product in Italy.

The Chinese government recently introduced

a 5 per cent chopstick tax to preserve its forests.

At Chinese funerals people sometimes burn paper money so the dead person will be rich in the after-life.

The Japanese language doesn't have genders but it does have different ways of speaking for men and women.

In 1982 an American man named David Grundman was killed by a cactus. It took some doing: he fired two shots from his shotgun at a giant saguaro cactus, which then fell on top of him.

The top six countries for the highest proportion of houses with five rooms or more are all English-speaking.

In Ethiopia, both males and females of the Surma tribes shave their heads as a mark of beauty.

A third of Africa's population survives on less than $1 a day.

In Alaska, one in 200 collisions between a car and a moose results in the death of a driver or passenger.

The Red Sea is the world's warmest sea, with an average temperature of 25 degrees Celsius.

A sultan's wife is called a sultana.

Wimbledon

Wimbledon was the world's very first tennis tournament.

200 spectators turned up to watch the first championship in 1877, paying one shilling each. The first champion, Spencer Gore, won 12 guineas.

Virginia Wade in 1977 and Andy Murray in 2016 were the last Britons to win the main Singles titles.

In the Second World War, a bomb fell on Centre Court, destroying most of the seating. The club remained open but was also used by various organizations, including the Home Guard.

Only five years have been entirely free of rain: 1931, 1976, 1977, 1993 and 1995.

Court 2 is known as 'The Graveyard' because it is where many seeded players have been knocked out.

Apart from jumpers/tracksuits etc., all players' clothing at the Wimbledon championships must be predominantly white. No other Grand Slam tournament has such a strict dress code for players.

The club colours, dark green and purple, were introduced in 1909.

Yellow balls were first used in 1986.

The tennis balls are stored at 20°C.

Every morning of the fortnight, one hour before the gates open, Hamish the hawk is released to ward off the local pigeons.

In 1985 17-year-old Boris Becker of Germany became the youngest player, the first unseeded player and the first German to win the Men's Singles.

Brame Hillyard, in 1930, was the first man to play wearing shorts rather than trousers.

Martina Navratilova holds the record for the most matches played by a woman: 326.

Jean Borotra holds the record for the most matches played by a man: 223. In 1964 he took part in the Men's Doubles at the age of 65.

Chairs were first provided for players to sit on between changing ends in 1975.

Lindsay Davenport, 1999 Ladies' Singles champion, is the tallest woman ever to compete at Wimbledon at 6 feet 2. At 4 feet 9, Gem Hoahing, who played in the late 1930s, was the shortest.

Only eight left-handers, six men and two women, have ever won a Wimbledon Singles title – the most recent being Goran Ivanisevic in 2001.

Martina Hingis (1994), Annabel Croft (1984), Tracy Austin (1978) and Ann Jones (as Ann Haydon in 1956) all won Girls' Singles titles.

In 2001 Goran Ivanisevic became the first wild card entrant to win a Singles title.

A wooden racket was last used at Wimbledon in 1987.

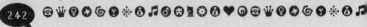

The London Underground

The London Underground is the longest and largest underground system in the world. It was also the world's first.

Number of miles travelled by each Tube train each year: 73,500.

Length of the network: 253 miles (408km).

More of the London Underground is above ground than under ground.

Proportion of the network that is in tunnels: 46 per cent.

Number of individual passengers carried on the Tube each year: 28 million.

Busiest stations: during the three-hour morning peak, London's busiest Tube station is Waterloo, with 51,100 people entering. The busiest station in terms of passengers each year is Victoria, with 76 million.

Passengers enter the Tube system at a rate of 146,000 people an hour.

Of the 287 stations on the London Underground, only 29 are south of the Thames.

Green grapes cause more accidents on the London Underground than banana skins.

The only British women singers who had US number ones

Leona Lewis: 'Bleeding Love' (2008)

The Spice Girls: 'Wannabe' (1997)

Kim Wilde: 'You Keep Me Hangin' On' (1987)

Bananarama: 'Venus' (1986)

Bonnie Tyler: 'Total Eclipse of the Heart' (1983)

Sheena Easton: 'Morning Train (9 to 5)' (1981)

Lulu: 'To Sir With Love' (1967)

Petula Clark: 'Downtown' (1965) and 'My Love' (1966)

Vera Lynn: 'Auf Wiederseh'n Sweetheart' (1952)

Books

The first book published is thought to be *The Epic of Gilgamesh*, written in about 3000BC in cuneiform, an alphabet based on symbols.

The first history book, *The Great Universal History*, was published by Rashid-Eddin of Persia in 1311.

In 1898 (14 years before the *Titanic* sank), Morgan Robertson wrote a novel called *Futility*. The story was about the largest ship ever built hitting an iceberg in the Atlantic Ocean.

Pope Benedict XVI had his library of 20,000 books photographed shelf by shelf so they could be reassembled in the Vatican in precisely the same order.

Scarlett O'Hara, the heroine of Margaret Mitchell's *Gone with the Wind*, was originally named Pansy.

In 1955 a book was returned to Cambridge University library – 288 years overdue.

The first draft of John Steinbeck's *Of Mice and Men* was eaten by his dog.

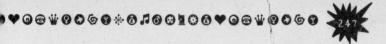

Bambi was originally published in 1929 in Germany.

Apart from the Bible, the world's most translated book is *Don Quixote*.

Leo Tolstoy's wife copied his manuscript of *War And Peace* seven times – by hand.

During the American Civil War, all the officers in the confederate army were given copies of *Les Misérables* by Victor Hugo to carry with them at all times because their leaders believed the book symbolized their cause.

Victor Hugo wrote *The Hunchback of Notre Dame* in six months – using (or so it is claimed) a single bottle of ink.

T. E. Lawrence (also known as Lawrence of Arabia) had to rewrite *Seven Pillars of Wisdom* – in full – after losing his only manuscript while changing trains at Reading station in 1919.

Things Said about books

'Books are for people who wish they were somewhere else.' (Mark Twain)

'The books you don't read can't help.' (Jim Rohn)

'A bookstore is one of the only pieces of evidence we have that people are still thinking.' (Jerry Seinfeld)

'You know you've read a good book when you turn the last page and feel a little as if you have lost a friend.' (Paul Sweeney)

'A room without books is like a body without a soul.' (Cicero)

Palindromes

A palindrome is a word or sentence that reads the same backwards or forwards.

A nut for a jar of tuna.

A Santa at NASA.

A Santa dog lived as a devil god at NASA.

A Santa lived as a devil at NASA.

A Toyota!

Race fast, safe car.

A dog! A panic in a pagoda!

A man, a pain, a mania – Panama.

Ana, nab a banana.

Anna: 'Did Otto peep?' Otto: 'Did Anna?'

Desserts, I stressed!

Did Hannah say as Hannah did?

Did I draw Della too tall, Edward? I did.

Do Good's deeds live on? No, Evil's deeds do, O God.

Do geese see god?

'Do nine men interpret?' 'Nine men,' I nod.

Draw putrid dirt upward.

Emil asleep, Hannah peels a lime.

Eva, can I stab bats in a cave?

Evade me, Dave.

Go deliver a dare, vile dog.

No, sir! Away! A papaya war is on.

No, sir, prefer prison.

No, it is opposition.

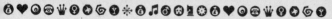

Some men interpret nine memos.

Too far, Edna, we wander afoot.

Too hot to hoot.

Was it a bar or a bat I saw?

Won't lovers revolt now?

Yawn a more Roman way!

American celebrities and their classmates' ratings:

Tom Cruise – voted Least Likely to Succeed

Sandra Bullock – voted Most Likely to Brighten Your Day

Halle Berry – voted Prom Queen

Chris Tucker – voted Most Humorous

Heather Graham – voted Most Talented

Kevin Federline – voted Most Likely to Be on *America's Most Wanted*

Ryan Philippe – voted Best Smile

Before fame

Keira Knightley was just three years old when she asked her parents if she could have an agent.

Jake Gyllenhaal worked as a lifeguard: 'Someone got stung by a jellyfish and I peed on the leg to counteract the sting.'

Nicole Richie's first puppy was a gift from Prince.

Owen Wilson got his bumpy nose after breaking it twice, once in a high school scuffle and once playing football with friends.

Lee Mead worked at KFC.

Lewis Hamilton was bullied at school because of his driving career.

Leonardo DiCaprio was fired from his first acting job for being disruptive. He was just five years old.

Hugh Jackman used to work the nightshift at a petrol station.

Katie Holmes loved Barbie and filled her bedroom with Barbie toys as a child.

Sylvester Stallone used to clean out lions' cages for a living.

As a boy, Ricky Gervais wanted to be a marine biologist.

Celebrity trivia

James McAvoy originally intended to be a missionary.

Robbie Williams, Kylie Minogue and Simon Cowell have all 'appeared' in *the Beano*

Jennifer Lopez insured her body for $1 billion.

Sir Elton John once said that if he had a daughter, he would call her 'Umbrella'.

Tom Cruise wore braces on his teeth as an adult.

Peter Kay once played a shopfitter in *Coronation Street*.

Jake Gyllenhaal's godmother is Jamie Lee Curtis.

Catherine Zeta Jones's parents won £100,000 at bingo.

re marrying Chris Martin from Coldplay,
Gwyneth Paltrow was engaged to Brad Pitt
and Ben Affleck.

Mariah Carey bought Marilyn Monroe's
childhood piano for more than $600,000 at
auction.

Sir Winston Churchill was an ordained druid.

Kanye West keeps koi carp (very expensive
ornamental fish).

John Cleese has a
species of lemur,
avahi Cleesei,
named after him.

Celebrities who launched their own products

Denise Van Outen – T-shirts

Christina Aguilera – perfume and cosmetics

Gwen Stefani – clothing

Missy Elliot – Misdemeanor Lipstick

Puff Daddy – clothing

Sienna Miller - clothing

Jennifer Lopez – clothing

Catherine Zeta Jones – baby clothes

Hilary Duff – clothes for dogs

Lily Allen – clothing

Kate Moss – clothing

Bats

90 per cent of all bats are microbats and weigh less than an ounce (28g).

Bats are voracious eaters – some devouring as many as 600 insects an hour through the night every night.

Baby bats are born upside down and are caught by their mothers' wings.

Bats can eat from one-half to three-quarters of their own body-weight in an evening.

Male epauletted bats have pouches in their shoulders that contain large patches of white fur, which they flash to attract mates.

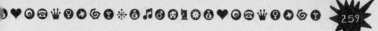

Britain's best-selling sandwich fillings

In order of popularity:

Chicken

Fish – mostly tuna and prawn

Cheese

Ham

Bacon

Egg

Sausage

For home-made sandwiches, cheese is the most popular choice, followed by ham, chicken, jam/sweet spreads, hot bacon and tuna.

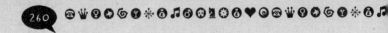

Aliases used by celebrities

Mr Bellacon – Tom Cruise

Sue Denim – Kylie Minogue

Mr Dripnoodle – Johnny Depp

Tipsy McStagger – Robbie Williams

Mr Tyne & Mr Wear – Ant and Dec

Claris Norman – Madonna

Sir Humphrey Handbag – Sir Elton John

Miss Cupcake – Mariah Carey

Marianne Antoinette – Mischa Barton

Famous people who own islands

Sir Richard Branson (Necker)

Leonardo DiCaprio (Blackadore Caye)

David Copperfield (Musha Cay)

United States

In the US, just three people together can be accused of rioting; in the UK, there have to be at least 12 people to create a riot.

One in every five New Yorkers was born in another country.

The American people together produce about 5,500kg of poo per second. Their livestock (cattle, pigs, sheep, etc.) produce more than 110,000kg of poo per second.

There's an organization in the state of Virginia called SCROOGE, which stands for Society to Curtail Ridiculous, Outrageous and Ostentatious Gift Exchanges. This was started to make present-giving affordable and simple.

Every year, 17 tons of gold is used to make wedding rings in the US.

Florida's beaches lose 20 million cubic yards of sand to the elements every year.

The state of Louisana was named after King Louis XIV of France.

It is estimated that 200,000,000 M&Ms are consumed each day in the US.

The Procrastinators' Club of America sends news to its members in 'last month's newsletter'.

The most popular name for a pet in the US is Max.

Every year, over 1,000 people are bitten by other people in New York City.

Every US bill – regardless of denomination – costs four cents to make.

The largest object ever found in the Los Angeles sewer system was a motorcycle.

80 per cent of American men say they would marry the same woman if they had to do it all over again.

50 per cent of American women say they would marry the same man if they had to do it all over again.

In an American Animal Hospital Association poll, 33 per cent of dog owners admitted that they talked to their dogs on the phone or left messages on an answering machine when they were away.
In the US, murder is committed most frequently in August and least frequently in February.

12 per cent of Americans believe that Joan of Arc was Noah's wife.

The Pentagon has 17.5 miles of corridors.

In 1994 the Los Angeles police arrested a man for dressing up as the Grim Reaper – complete with scythe – and standing outside the windows of old people's homes, staring in.

About 7 million cars are scrapped each year in the US.

The venture capital arm of the CIA is named 'In-Q-Tel' in honour of Q from the James Bond books and films.

Some visitors to Las Vegas are so overweight that the emergency services have invested in a fleet of special ambulances equipped with a winch to deal with them. In six months, medics had to pick up 75 patients who weighed over 225kg.

There are over 60 towns in US where the word 'turkey' appears in the name.

Many businesses in Nebraska are prefaced by the word 'Aksarben'. Aksarben is Nebraska spelled backwards.

Every year, more Frisbee discs are sold in the US than baseballs, basketballs and footballs combined.

In 2006 an American man named Eric Dogan left Amanda Newkirk, a waitress, a tip of $973.65 on a $24.35 bill.

Every US state has a state butterfly.

Famous best friends

Holly Willoughby and Fearne Cotton

Ashley Tisdale and Miley Cyrus

Liv Tyler and Stella McCartney

Myleene Klass and Suzanne Shaw

Nicole Kidman and Naomi Watts

Ben Affleck and Matt Damon

Courtney Cox and Jennifer Aniston

Penélope Cruz and Salma Hayek

Famous left-handers

Prince William

Drew Barrymore

Eminem

Robert De Niro

George Michael

Tom Cruise

John McEnroe

Julia Roberts

Ross Kemp

Accomplished roller-bladers

Tom Cruise

Dustin Hoffman

Nicole Kidman

Robbie Williams

Phillip Schofield

Bruce Willis

Madonna

Played themselves on *The Simpsons*

Sir Paul McCartney

Britney Spears

Professor Stephen Hawking

Mel Gibson

Jerry Springer

Sir Elton John

Bono

Sir Mick Jagger

J. K. Rowling

50 Cent

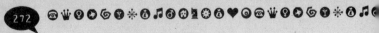

Famous last words

'Hold the cross high so I may see it through the flames!' (Joan of Arc, 1431)

'All my possessions for a moment of time.' (Queen Elizabeth I, 1603)

'I'm still alive.' (The Emperor Caligula, AD 41)

'Tomorrow, I shall no longer be here.' (Nostradamus – possibly the only prophecy he got right, 1566)

'Friends, applaud, the comedy is over.' (Ludwig van Beethoven, 1827)

'Go on, get out! Last words are for fools who haven't said enough.' (Karl Marx, 1883)

'If this is dying, I don't think much of it.' (Lytton Strachey, 1932)

'Never felt better.' (Douglas Fairbanks Sr, 1939)

'Dying is a very dull affair. My advice to you is to have nothing whatever to do with it.'
(W. Somerset Maugham, 1965)

'It hurts.' (Charles de Gaulle, 1970)

Mitchell Symons
HOW TO AVOID A WOMBAT'S BUM*
And other fascinating facts!

* Don't chase it! Wombats can run up to 25 miles per hour and stop dead in half a stride. They kill their predators this way – the predator runs into the wombat's bum-bone and smashes its face.

Amaze and intrigue your friends and family with more fantastic facts and figures:

- most dinosaurs were no bigger than chickens
- Everton was the first British football club to introduce a stripe down the side of players' shorts
- A snail has about 25,000 teeth
- No piece of paper can be folded in half more than seven times

Just opening this book will have you hooked for hours!

Mitchell Symons
WHY EATING BOGEYS IS GOOD FOR YOU
And other crazy facts explained!

Ever wondered . . .

- Why we have tonsils?
- Is there any cream in cream crackers?
- What's the best way to cure hiccups?
- And if kangaroos keep their babies in their pouches, what happens to all the poo?

Mitchell Symons answers all these wacky questions and plenty more in a wonderfully addictive book that will have you hooked for hours!

(And eating bogeys is good for you . . . but only your own!)

Selected for the Booktrust Booked Up! Initiative in 2008.

MITCHELL SYMONS
How much **poo** does an **ELEPHANT** do?*
...and further fascinating facts!

Mitchell Symons
HOW MUCH POO DOES AN ELEPHANT DO?*
And further fascinating facts!

* an elephant produces an eye-wateringly pongy 20 kilos of dung a day!

Let Mitchell Symons be your guide into the weird and wonderful world of trivia.

- Camels are born without humps
- Walt Disney, creator of Mickey Mouse, was scared of mice
- Only 30% of humans can flare their nostrils
- A group of twelve or more cows is called a flink

Mitchell Symons
WHY DO FARTS SMELL LIKE ROTTEN EGGS?*

And more crazy facts explained!

Ever wondered . . .

- Why we burp?
- What a wotsit is?
- Whether lemmings really jump off cliffs?
- Why vomit always contains carrots?
- And why do farts smell like rotten eggs?

No subject is too strange and no trivia too tough for Mitchell Symons, who has the answers to these crazy questions, and many more.